LOVE UNKNOWN

LOVE UNKNOWN

THE ARCHBISHOP OF CANTERBURY'S LENT BOOK 2012

RUTH BURROWS OCD

continuum

Published by the Continuum International Publishing Group

The Tower Building
11 York Road
London
SE1 7NX

80 Maiden Lane
Suite 704
New York
NY 10038

www.continuumbooks.com

First published 2011

British Library Cataloguing-in-Publication Data
A catalogue record for this book is available from the British Library.

ISBN: PB: 978-1-4411-0372-7

Designed and typeset by Fakenham Prepress Solutions, Fakenham, Norfolk NR21 8NN

Printed and bound in India

Sing to God a song you have never sung
before!
O earth, raise aloud your singing voice!
Where his eyes rest there is beauty and
brightness:
in his holy presence, all is holy and lovely.

cf. Ps. 96(95):1.6

—

CONTENTS

FOREWORD BY THE ARCHBISHOP OF CANTERBURY

There is all the difference in the world between having a "spiritual life" and walking in the way of Jesus. Throughout her long life as a Carmelite sister, Ruth Burrows has returned many times to this crucial theme, and in this book she offers a wonderfully vivid and direct statement of the challenge. If we want to be disciples of Jesus – not interested onlookers, not more or less enthusiastic subscribers to a spiritual method, but actual disciples – we have to get used to uprooting quite a few habits of thought; and what we shall encounter here is a careful and loving diagnosis of the most damaging of those habits, in the light of the plain story of Scripture.

The heart of the problem, we are told, is in the way we inherit false and enslaving pictures of

God. We receive and internalize the idea that God is jealous of us, suspicious of us, out to make our lives difficult – so we become in turn jealous and suspicious, and make our own lives and those of all around us difficult. We act as if we had to impress God, as if we had to have something in our "repertoire" that would guarantee that he would take us seriously – so we build up a professional arsenal of spiritual riches that will secure our place with him.

But the God of the Bible, and above all the God of Jesus, is not our rival or our examiner or our prosecutor but our lover. There is nothing we can do to impress him or put him in our debt. If we start from the assumption that we have to do these things, we shall become either deludedly arrogant or despairing. If we allow ourselves to be lured out of these fictions and prisons, we see that our utter inability to acquire a satisfactory and impressive spiritual life is the best possible news, because then we can simply put ourselves in his hands, trusting his love. When we are empty of our fantasies about goodness or holiness or integration or however we phrase it, we can just allow God to be who he is – "love unknown", the one who wants to live in us and pray in us, so that we – silenced and humbled by his generosity – can come to life again, without anxiety, without arrogance, without despair.

Ruth Burrows takes us on a journey through the biblical narrative in lucid, accessible terms, to show how this awareness of God as gift and lover comes to birth in the experience of God's people and is made clear and effective once and for all in Jesus, so that the blockage of our frantic self-obsession is at last broken by his Spirit. It does not mean that ahead there lies a life of easy confidence and surface peace. Quite the opposite in fact. It does mean that our dry and dull inner life, the brick walls we face, the sense of getting nowhere are all acknowledged without panic because the focus is God's action, not ours. And, ultimately, to be a disciple is to let God in Jesus Christ be who he is, free from our fuss and fear or our hopes for impressive personal holiness. As the Bible says, Jesus is our holiness and all we can do is let him live in us.

So often in her writings, Ruth Burrows helps us see once again the fundamentals of our faith. In these pages, she distils, movingly and personally, a lifetime of discovering the God who is greater than our "religious" aspirations, greater than our fears and our hopes alike – the Biblical God who is who he is and will be who he will be, who lives and works eternally as though there were nothing more important in the universe than us, his confused, unimpressive, self-deluding, unfathomably loveable creatures.

+Rowan Cantuar

PREFACE

On receiving the request to write the Archbishop of Canterbury's Book for Lent, what should swim into my mind but Robert Burn's lines addressed to the "sleekit", "tim'rous beastie", whose nest his plough had invaded. O what a panic's in my breastie! My great regard for the Archbishop, who, I was informed by the wily editor, really wanted me to do it, put no small pressure on my emotions, but I was anxious.

"*Could* I do it?" I never think of myself as a writer. I have happened to write a few books, because from time to time I felt I had something to say; the matter was already there, and I was never tied to time. A year might seem long enough for completing a small book, but I belong to a community and my time is not my own. Our day is tightly scheduled with many hours devoted to prayer, and each of us must shoulder her share of what is involved in the maintenance of a large household. I can never, from day to day, be sure of having time for writing. However, allowing myself a few days in which to pray and reflect,

I conclude that I should do it. So the panic in my breastie has subsided and I commit myself willingly to this task. I must trust in the guidance of the Holy Spirit as to what to offer to my Anglican brothers and sisters.

INTRODUCTION

It is an abiding grief to me that many faithful religious people, even regular churchgoers, understand little of the great truths they sincerely profess to believe. My special grief is for our young people. As children, they accompany their parents to church and delight in what goes on, perhaps active in the liturgy as acolytes and servers. But unless a real love for Jesus is awakened in their hearts, unless they have been helped to perceive something of the wonder and sheer beauty of the content of the faith in which they are instructed, how can they withstand the atheism of our materialistic society? It is in the very air they must breathe.

Recently I was saddened on reading a letter from a young man I have known since he was a schoolboy and is now a husband, and father of three infants. He writes: "I am frightened. Much of what I believed in my life is crumbling. A religion I once held dear no longer makes sense to me." The word "religion" is significant. There is a vast difference between religion and faith in the God revealed in Jesus Christ, or, as a dear friend of mine expresses it, there is a vast difference between being religious and being a true disciple of Jesus. In the first instance, being a faithful Christian seems to consist in living a good moral life, practising justice and love towards others, and faithfully observing certain religious practices. Praise indeed, for those who live so! They are precious to God and he longs to give them so much more. The inner disturbance and distress this young man is feeling could well be the secret call of the Spirit to go beyond the externals to a purer, deeper faith, to an encounter, mysterious by its very nature, with the living and true God revealed in Jesus Christ.

Often and often I have reflected on what can be done to ensure the seismic shift from being just religious to ardent discipleship. Does it rest entirely on zealous teaching, preaching or even example? It seems not. Those of us, who by God's mercy may claim that they really *desire* to be disciples, can no doubt recall the "moment" when in some way they saw, or more truly they were shown, they were awakened. The "moment" may have been an extended moment or a stunning lightning flash. Dramatic or not, the heart of it was: I wàs blind and now I see. God really matters!

We know that we must change, that much in our conduct and attitudes is not good.

Responding thus to this new vision, which is nothing less than an encounter with the Lord, is what he means by, "Do penance, for the kingdom of God is at hand." How profound, how precious a grace! It is indeed the pearl of great price. Why is it given to some and not to others? We do not know. Listening to the stories of aspirants to our monastery I have discerned no pattern. This one comes from an explicitly atheistic family, educated to be a very moral atheist, while that one comes from nominal Christianity and religious indifference. Rare today is one whose childhood faith and practice have matured along with her natural growth, and then found her vocation as a Carmelite. When I have been told these stories of conversion and read of others, I know that I am confronted with miracles of grace for which one can only give thanks.

Why is it that, in a devout family, some of the children remain steadfast in faith and others do not? Why does one young person show signs of more than ordinary spiritual insight and spiritual desire? We simply do not know. Is the offer made to all in varying degrees and in various guises, but ignored by some or even knowingly and wilfully rejected? Again, we do not know. Jesus gives us the parable of the seed lavishly sown, which clearly indicates the part played by human responsibility in the seed's fruitfulness. However, there are many texts to infer invincible human ignorance and therefore lack of responsibility in individuals. It is the disciples' task to do something about this: "[H]ow are they to believe in him of whom they have not heard (have never been shown what he is like)? And how are they to hear without a preacher?" (Rom. 10:14). Again, "Let your light so shine before men, that they may see your good works and give glory to your Father, who is in heaven" (Matt. 5:16). What is more, Jesus makes it clear in his picture of the judgment (Matt. 25), that many know, love and serve him without knowing his name. The human heart is God's most secret domain. We may never judge another because we simply cannot.

What we must be certain of is that the pure, totally unmerited grace we have received, if it is indeed the pearl of great price to be guarded with our very life, is a talent that must be put to use. It is not given for ourselves alone but for others. To be a Christian is to be a missionary. A Christian is one "sent". In one way or another, according to the varied ministries assigned to each one of us, we must live, not for ourselves, but for others. The lives of each of us interlock; how I live affects all; how others live affects me. "Thy kingdom come, thy will be done on earth as it is in heaven." Our Creator has one great plan for his cherished creatures, a plan of unimaginable blessedness such as "no eye has seen, nor ear heard, nor the heart of man conceived" prepared for those who love him (1 Cor. 2:9). This vocation to untold blessedness which is "thy will", is conceived "in heaven", that is, in the depths of God's heart before the foundation of the world. To cooperate with God in his great work of universal saving love must be our willed – not necessarily felt – desire and aim. Only those called to be true disciples will be reading this little book and it is to these that it is directed and dedicated. Maybe someone is thinking sadly: "I have received no call. I wish I had." Be certain that to think it, to want it, is the call. His loving gaze rests on you. You have no excuse. Gird your loins and follow the Lord!

We must, each one of us, go on praying for what God wants to give us. If we ourselves would lavish on our children everything that is good for them, "how much more will the heavenly Father give the Holy Spirit to those who ask him?" (Luke 11:13). The work of the Holy Spirit, the Spirit of holiness from heaven, is to conform us to Jesus, to make our Lord's saving presence ever deeper, more effective in this world through us insofar as his kingdom comes in us, insofar as each of us is possessed by his Spirit. Personal holiness is the most real, the indispensable apostolate. Holiness can never be acquired. Holiness is "from heaven"; it is the marvellous work of the divine Spirit in the man or woman who invites it and surrenders to it.

For over 70 years I have been trying to become a true disciple of Jesus, my beloved Lord. I have prayed, I have pored over the gospels, reflected long and hard, trying to discern the divine will and guidance in everything in my life, and now I am asked to share what I understand. With Paul I can say: "Not that I have already obtained or am already perfect; but I press on" (Phil. 3:12).

ONE

The Only Saviour

Do not be afraid, daughter of Sion.
See! I am coming,
I, your Saviour.

These words from Matins of the second Sunday of Advent of 1942, dropped into my desolate 19-year-old heart as the word of God to me. In the wake of a powerful grace, I had entered the Carmelite monastery 14 months earlier and during that time every vestige of spiritual pretension had been swept clean away. Not that I had enjoyed any illusions in regard to my spiritual life before I entered, but I cherished a fervent hope that a year in Carmel would produce some fair blooms of holiness if not complete transformation! Alas, alas! I was vividly, painfully aware that I was selfish to the core and everything a Carmelite should not be. I had imbibed an image of what was expected of a Carmelite.

She should be aflame with love for God. I was stone cold.

She should want suffering and be good at bearing it. I shunned it and was bad at bearing it.

No angry, resentful, envious, mean, competitive thoughts and impulses should sully a mind and heart given to God. I had all these things in abundance.

A Carmelite loved all the observances of the life. I found most of them boring and some made me angry as I felt they impinged on my dignity.

A Carmelite loved nothing better than solitude, to be alone with God alone. I wanted love, interest, variety; I wanted lots of things!

In short, I felt I was a sham, pretending to be something I was not. I lacked a natural religious sense and feared I was an agnostic if not an atheist at heart.

My purpose in being autobiographical is simply to tell you how I came to have an indestructible conviction that the weaker, the more wretched and poor we are, the more we realize that we have no goodness of our own, and cleave to Jesus with might and main, taking him absolutely at his word that he has come to save sinners, that he has come as our servant, our healer, the more is he able to do everything for us.

Looking back over my long life in Carmel – 70 years so far – I believe I can appraise it with reasonable objectivity. It seems to me that it was in the direct divine plan that I should experience the absoluteness of God from the very start. It must be pointed out that many of the observances of the Order during the first 20 or more years of my life as a nun were wholly inappropriate and potentially dangerous. This is not to impugn the good intentions and dedicated love of those who upheld them.

These observances derived from the culture of late sixteenth and early seventeen-century Europe and no doubt were life nurturing to the religious of that time and place, but they were not beneficent to English women of the early and middle twentieth century. My temperament is hardly ideal for the purely contemplative enclosed life at the best of times, but given the circumstances prevailing in my youth, it is not surprising that there were plenty of outbursts and tears.

Yet I do not regret the many years passed under that hard, testing regime. I gained enormous experience, an experience that proved invaluable when it fell to me to implement the norms for the updating of enclosed religious life following the second Vatican Council. Human needs were to be recognized and provided for, but how essential it was that, in re-forming a way of life, in catering for proper human needs, we should not thereby sacrifice the essence of Carmel which I understand to be in very truth the poor ones, standing nakedly exposed to God, with nothing to offer him but their need and emptiness.

It seems to me that God wanted me to understand the Carmelite charism in a very profound way. The circumstances I have described contributed to this. It is easy to vaunt one's "poverty", "wretchedness", and so forth, but truly, I cannot convey how unremitting and painful was the awareness of my sinfulness and spiritual helplessness. On the level of normal perception, I was a complete failure. It would have been impossible to communicate the reality of it to another, even had I dared to do so!

Although on the ordinary level of consciousness, I had no sense whatever of God's nearness and still less of his love, I never ceased clinging to him. Like a drowning person clinging to a spar, I hung on. I claimed him as my absolute Saviour, fully aware that I had no other.

I recall an anecdote I heard during the war. The anti-aircraft guns were blasting away into the sky and a little girl exclaimed: "Oh, I do hope they don't hit God because if they do we're sunk." Well, if my clinging prayer was not heard, then not only I but all of us are "sunk"! The God Jesus revealed would not be God and Jesus, blessed Jesus, would be proved a fake! Never, never!

It must be said that I was always earnestly trying to do what was pleasing to our Lord, but often enough my selfishness and temperament got the better of me. However, I never "threw in the towel", never indulged – as my temperament wanted to – in spiritual "sulks" but humbled myself before our Lord and asked for help. A saying of our founding mother, St Teresa of Avila, became a key word for me: "Humility is the ointment for all our wounds." I believe that I really wanted to know the truth, no matter how painful.

I was blessed in that, almost from the beginning of my serious discipleship, the New Testament opened up to me and the Jesus I found there, what he said, what he did, the way he was, became the rock on which I built my house. Totally dissatisfied with myself, aware of deeply ingrained sinful tendencies, I identified with the leper kneeling before Jesus, begging to be healed. Aware of how blind I was, I prayed for sight. Although I had no emotional, sensible awareness of any relationship with Jesus, I believed. I *chose* to take with utmost seriousness his assurance that to ask is to receive, to seek is to find, to knock is to have the door opened.

My favourite, most reassuring piece of scripture was the story of the prodigal son. Often and often I saw myself as that prodigal, like him unkempt and soiled, but unlike him, I rushed into the Father's embrace asking him to love me all the more and be more extravagantly good to me. At times of great despondency I would, so to speak, rehearse to Jesus just how I saw myself, how I had nothing within myself to reassure me, how unloving and selfish I was, and, of course, I would, in faith, receive my answer: he threw his arms around my neck and kissed me (cf. Luke 15:20).

In this way, I struggled, stumbled on, down the years, with no sense of achievement, no awareness of drawing closer to God, no emotional comfort.

And yet, deep down within, too far down for me to enjoy, was a secret wisdom. It was showing me that I was experiencing the reality of being a human being, "man", not God, that I was living in truth, exposed to the absolute God and to no human idol. To be exposed to such light and love even when experienced as absence, non-love, darkness, is to see every impurity, see how far, far away we are from the purity, the holiness of God. "Depart from me, for I am a sinful woman" (cf. Luke 5:8).

Although I might feel like crying that, I would not do so because I knew he wanted to be near me, and I knew that only he could purify me in his own holiness. Of course, I am looking down the tunnel of years at my young self, and interpreting her experience in a way she could not have done at the time.

Mysteriously, however, I "knew". It was this infused faith reinforcing my own stubborn *choosing* to believe that enabled me to go on steadfastly.

What is more, I found that, although I prayed ardently to love, to understand, to be faithful and so forth, I always added the rider that it was the reality I was asking for not the comfort of knowing and feeling that I loved, or that I was faithful. I was not asking for a light I could appreciate but only that light he wished me to have. I longed and prayed to be wholly faithful yet have never felt that I am.

"No one can understand Carmel except those who live it", we exclaim with feeling to one another. All sorts of romantic image are abroad. One sees beautiful photographs of serenity: a nun sitting in the orchard reading, walking down an avenue of trees, working tranquilly in kitchen, garden or at her computer. Visitors attend our liturgies and testify to the atmosphere of peace and prayer. Not for one moment do I deny the reality of these qualities but no one can know the depths of experience in which they are forged. From the outside, it can seem as if we have removed ourselves from the stresses and heavy responsibilities of normal human life.

That is true to some extent and we ourselves never forget it. However, in the measure that we really embrace the life of Carmel, we know we are carrying great responsibilities for the world. We experience in an almost naked way what it is to be human in a fallen world. Carmel reduces life to its basics.

This was far more obvious in the first two decades of my life. Then it was indeed a desert with almost nothing on the human level to interest, to comfort – at least, that is how I experienced it. Unless the measures undertaken to adapt to modern life have radically changed the way of life, those who really come to grips with the vocation, experience the human vocation in a deep way and live face to face with their native, essential poverty. The façades we humans erect to protect our fragility, like the walls of Jericho come tumbling down.

Human poverty is a deep mystery that plunges us into Trinitarian depths. At the moment I am dwelling only on the actual, quite homely way we come up against our poverty, and by that I mean our experience of sinfulness, weakness, and in general our limitations of one kind and another, and to suggest how, practically, we might embrace it as our Lord would wish us to. Is there one of us who has not, at some time or other, been forced to look in the glass of self-knowledge at an unflattering image? We cannot live with other people and not get our corners knocked off. The trouble is that we do not use this grace – for grace it is – as we ought.

We allow ourselves to resent criticism even when justified. Note that I say *allow* – the *feeling* of resentment is not within our control – and maybe we try to smudge the unpalatable truth by discrediting the critic and, should an opportunity arise, retaliate in kind. Perhaps we run to someone on whom we can count to soothe our hurt, to reassure and rehabilitate us. The same sort of escape routes are taken when, in one way or another, we fail in our own eyes or in the eyes of others. What opportunities for growth we disciples of Jesus miss by not giving proper value to these commonplace occurrences!

St Teresa assures her Carmelite sisters that one day of humbling self-knowledge – she has in mind days of stress when, in close relationships with others, our nerves are set on edge and our tempers frayed and we see ourselves as we are, selfish, unloving creatures – one such day, she says, is of far greater value than hours spent in meditation. Our days are strewn with graces that we do not recognize: opportunities, for instance, of letting another take precedence or receive the credit for something we ourselves have said or done; of refraining from profuse excuses when we have made mistakes and shown ourselves incompetent. A thousand and one things happen that wound our self-love. Let be, let be!

If only we really knew Jesus we would not be so concerned with putting on a good show and of how others see us. Instead of concealing our insecurities, fears, secret failings even from our selves, we would accept the reality that we are, tranquil in the certainty that our Lord looks on us with infinite compassion and love.

It is so difficult for us to grasp the reality of the Incarnation: the truth that our great God, our holy Creator, has, so we may say, thrown off his robes of grandeur and run out in eagerness to meet us, to be with us where we are. There are promises of this in the Old Testament: "I will dwell in your midst," "Emmanuel". It is simply too good to be true! It just can't be true! But it *is* true. I know no writer who has so conveyed to us the tender, incredible nearness of our Lord to us as Julian of Norwich: "He that is highest and mightiest, noblest and worthiest, is lowest and meekest, homeliest and most courteous."[1] "For our soul is so preciously loved of Him that is highest, that it overpasseth the knowing of all creatures: that is to say, there is no creature that

13

is made that may fully know how much and how sweetly and how tenderly our Maker loveth us."[2] Many other exquisite expressions of the intimate quality of our Lover's love for us could be cited. The title of her book could justifiably read: "Revelations of the Tenderness and Courtesy of Divine Love". If we would constantly ponder on this nearness – not ask to feel it but to believe it – all our anxieties about our relationship with God would melt away. We would cease to fret because "I can't pray"; "prayer doesn't work for me", and wail over similar experiences of our helplessness.

Centuries before God came to us as one of us, the prophet, Second Isaiah, discerned a yearning tenderness in the Holy One of Israel, the One to whom the Cherubim unceasingly sang: "Holy, holy, holy is the Lord God of Hosts. Heaven and earth are full of your glory" (cf. Is. 6:3). "God has forgotten us. Our God in whom we put our trust has been shown up as powerless before the gods of Babylon. Nothing will ever change", wailed the exiles in Babylon. The prophet rallies them, vaunting the power and majesty of the Creator God, Israel's God, revealed in his creation.

14

Powerless? Who but he has the measure of all things, the waters, the mountains, the very dust of the earth? His wisdom, his knowledge, his power are beyond question. Look up to the starry firmament! – vista of unearthly beauty and mystery. They must have wondered as they gazed at myriad glittering beings, aloof, enigmatic, unlike the things of earth and water, totally beyond their reach. The God of Israel is their Lord, "he brings out their host in number, calling them all by name and because of the greatness of his might, and because he is strong in power not one is missing" (Is. 40:26).

From consideration of God's majesty and power, he brings down their gaze to the familiar, infinitely tender sight of a young mother suckling her baby: "Can a woman forget her sucking child, that she should have no compassion on the son of her womb? Even if she should forget, yet I will not forget you" (Is. 49:15).

It is Isaiah, too, who gives us the image of a shepherd leading home his flock, carrying the little ones in his bosom, tenderly caring for the pregnant ewes. But one greater than any prophet reveals to us the tenderness of God towards his wayward, weak, sinful children: "I have pity on them", not "I condemn them" (cf. Matt. 9:36; Mark 6:34). "Jerusalem, Jerusalem ...! How often would I have gathered your children together as a hen gathers her brood under her wing" (Matt. 23:37). What greater nearness than this? In his earthly life, as a male, he could not, of course, give full expression to his human tenderness, but it is evident and those who loved him were fully aware of it. Mark tells us that he caressed little children and held them in his arms (Mark 9:36; 10:16). It is of the utmost importance that we really *know* our God and how can we know him truly except through the closest attention to Jesus himself and to those whose words and deeds are consonant with his?

Although our daily lives bring us countless opportunities for confronting our limitations and moral failings, it is in prayer especially that they will be revealed. The prayer I have in mind is non-active. It is putting aside a period of time that is exclusively for God. Its basic is faith in God's loving presence to me, faith in his desire to be all mine; it is an entreaty, a desire that he should look at me with his tender pity, a looking that will burn away every impurity, and implant in me all he desires.

"Thy kingdom come in me, thy will be done in me." The heart, the deep reality of this prayer is the self-giving God: "My Father is ever at work" (John 5:17). What is this "work" but the giving of eternal life, that life which is God's own life and that takes us up into the divine family? Ah, but we are not allowed to see this – we *cannot* as yet see it – we must *believe* and stay exposed, surrendered in faith.

We shall want to run away because we are likely to see not the adorable face of Jesus but our own dirty face. We shall find it so, so difficult to remain in faith and find all sorts of excuse for not giving the time or for cutting it short. How bitterly I have experienced this helplessness in prayer throughout my long contemplative life.

As Carmelites, prayer is our life; prayer is our principle work for the Church and for the world. *We have nothing else!* Think what it is for a Carmelite to feel such a failure at prayer, not just now and then, but day after day, year after year! I lived with this searing anxiety for many, many years.

I remember especially when the work of Mother Teresa of Calcutta among the poor outcasts of

Calcutta first came to our knowledge. It was a sword in my heart. What love! What true service of our Lord! What is my life compared with hers? What am I doing for him, for his poor and outcasts? In this searching pain, I spontaneously wrote:

My brothers wander in the dark,
how bring them to the Light of life,
how bring them to your flame?
I look with wonder,
yes, sometimes with envy,
on that servant of the outcast tending
    you in them.
But deep within my heart I know
another way is mine:
in silence and alone,
living at the source of life – your heart,
in constant prayer, complete surrender.
Fill me, Lord, that I may overflow,
yet emptied first.
caverns …
        yearnings.

My cries you've heard, my tears you've
    known.
How deeply we live, we hidden ones!

Freed from the anguish and storms of
    life?
Lord, you know!

Children of our age we bear its burdens,
share its grief,
gather it up, day by day and give it to
    you.
So day by day we bless you,
day by day we celebrate, singing your
    praise,
breaking your bread in love and
    fellowship.

We come to meet you
as you come to us.
Here we are Lord,
for you.

"I prayed, and understanding was given
    me,
I called upon God and the spirit of
    wisdom came to me." (Wis. 7:7)

I understood that, with divine passion, God
wants to love us to fulfilment, and I understood
that for this to happen we must surrender to him

every single key of the kingdom of self. I understood that, without realizing it, our spiritual life
is as often as not self-seeking. We are intent on
creating a beautiful self into which God will be
privileged to enter! We want to feel we are good,
pure and holy; we want to be lifted up out of the
drab reality of our human condition. We want a
holiness of our own. I understood that God, in
his love, must destroy all this self-seeking and
that our happiness depends on our allowing him
to do so.

Two

If You Knew the Gift of God

O holy Jesus, most merciful redeemer,
friend and brother,
may I know thee more clearly,
love thee more dearly
and follow thee more nearly.
Amen.[3]

We are Christians, believers in God – not in any god, but in the God whom Jesus called Father. We are the redeemed, the Easter People, so, in examining the content of our faith, we are not out to prove anything but only to deepen our knowledge and love of God. "My heart is ever crying out to you, show me your face" (Ps. 27(26):8). It is our longing for God that leads us to think theologically. We want to contemplate the face of the Beloved, to trace every feature, to read every line of it, so as to know him as he really is and love and worship him in truth. Revelation is not mere information. Revelation is God disclosing his intimate self to us as a lover to his beloved. We are loved, cherished, honoured, blessed beyond belief. Can we bring home to ourselves that the great and holy God actually woos us? Only after long, long years am I beginning to assimilate the truth that God really, really wants our love as a human lover really, really wants the love of his beloved. Yes, he woos us as a shy, humble youth woos the girl who has captured his heart. Can you believe it? Dare we say that God needs our love for his happiness?

When we love someone, we want to know all we possibly can about them. We want to know

of their parentage, of their childhood and everything that has happened in their life. We want to
enter into their heart, to understand and share
their interests, their joys, their sorrows. For that
reason, we seek information. Similarly, our desire
to love God will mean that we try to gain as full an
intellectual knowledge of God as lies within our
power as individuals, pondering the revelation of
God contained in scripture and in the dogmas
our faith enunciated in the Creeds. We have to
bear in mind that dogma and even the words
of scripture are not in themselves revelation but
doors opening onto the inexhaustible Truth, the
holy Mystery. *The* door, as Jesus tells us, is Jesus.

"*Think* of the love the Father has for us that we
should be called children of God; and so we are"
(1 John 3:1). St Paul prays that "the Father of
our Lord Jesus Christ, the Father of glory, may
give you a spirit of wisdom and of revelation in
the knowledge of him, having the eyes of your
hearts enlightened" (Eph.1:17–18), Paul, who
had been thrown to the ground, his whole way
of seeing things overturned, his whole being
impassioned by what was shown him on the
Damascus road. He wants us, too, to realize
something of what God offers, of the glorious

destiny that is ours. Surely, with Paul and all the other great lovers of Christ, we want to glimpse something of "the breadth and length and height and depth of the love of Christ which surpasses all knowledge" (Eph. 3:18–19), an unfathomable ocean, a mine of inexhaustible riches. In the measure that we see (in faith), so shall we be moved to trust, to surrender in love to our divine Lover. The Church gives us the season of Lent as a special time for reflection in preparation for our celebration of the climax of revelation: the death and resurrection of our Saviour.

We can, I think, gain in perception, reverence and gratitude if we stand back a little from the treasure we possess and ask ourselves a few questions. Can we really know God? Is not God inconceivable to us, utterly beyond the bounds of our human faculties, a horizon that is ever dissolving before our straining inward eyes? We are told in scripture that no one can see God and live. Is it not presumptuous as well as futile to attempt to soar to this light, to dare the dwelling of this death-dealing reality? Yes, it is – presumptuous and futile. Yet, to the question, "Can we know God?" the answer is yes, we can and we do, because God has chosen to reveal himself, has shown himself as wanting to be known. We know God through the human life of God: the life, death and resurrection of Jesus Christ. Jesus' history, his life, his death are nothing less than the human life and death of God. Here lies our true vision of God. Here is revealed the living God, a Mystery of triune love, by whom, through whom, in whom everything exists. There is no "outside" of this Mystery, no thing whatsoever of independent existence: this Mystery encompasses and penetrates all, and we learn that it is absolute, self-giving love. Rightly is it said that the Crucified One, stretched out on the cross, "emptied" of all that we think of as human beauty and dignity, "a worm and no man" (Ps. 22(21):6) is our truest image of God. Mysterious assertion!

It is the Spirit whom the glorified Christ sends to us who reveals this mystery to us, who throws radiant light on the cross: "See, your God, your Lover! See, he gives you all he is, holding nothing back. Look upon an utterly self-giving love and know that this is your God." Such was the experience of that great theologian, Julian of Norwich, in her first "Showing". It was precisely when she was gazing at the suffering, bleeding head of Jesus crowned with thorns that suddenly, the Trinity filled her with utmost joy. "And so I understood", she writes, "it will be in heaven without end to all those who come there. For the Trinity is God: God is the Trinity; the Trinity is our Maker and Keeper, the Trinity is our everlasting joy and bliss, by our Lord Jesus Christ … for where Jesus appeareth, the blessed Trinity is understood, as to "my sight.""[4]

Some people claim that we can have knowledge of God apart from Jesus. It is true that, in the measure that we are alert, we are aware of living in mystery. Some have a stronger sense of this than others. It can be a joyful, reassuring experience, but equally it can be one of loneliness, emptiness, and seemingly meaninglessness. Always it raises questions that we can strive to answer or choose to ignore. Moreover, we have a conscience and instinctively know that we are answerable – to whom, to what? I have heard several people tell me that they have communion with a loving God and do not need Jesus. They have no need of a church; they find God in nature and pray to him there. Well, of our very nature we are creatures of desire. We lack. We want. We long for love, for beauty, for truth, for happiness, as the hart longs for flowing streams. We have a deep conviction that we are meant to be happy. Why should we feel this unless perfect happiness is there for us somewhere? This "hope does not deceive us, because God's love has been poured into our hearts by the Holy Spirit who has been given to us" (Rom. 5:5), and this Holy Spirit flows from the pierced heart of the crucified Christ. Whether we believe it or not, we are all graced. Every one of us has been taken over Jordan into the Promised Land and tastes some of its fruits. Do those people who find their God in the wonders and beauties of creation face up to nature's cruelties? Be that as it may, my concern here and now is with "my even-Christians, that well, well beloved people",[5] to use Julian's sweet expression, with those who believe with me that Jesus is our Way, our Truth, our Life, and believe his own words: "No one can come to the Father except through me" (John 14:6).

The first Christians, whose thinking is reflected in the writers of the New Testament, were continually pondering on the Jesus who had lived among them, as one of them, to whom they had listened, had gazed upon, and touched with their hands; the Jesus whom they dared hope was the longed-for Messiah, only to experience the shattering of this hope when they saw him utterly defeated, humiliated beyond measure, cruelly killed, "dead and buried", and finally were experiencing him not as one resuscitated merely but as one living with a hitherto inconceivable life, exalted, empowered, invisible, but vitally present.

Very soon they could refer to him as Son in a mysterious, profound way unknown to their tradition. He was Son equal to the Father, the Holy One of Israel. Jesus, it was clear, was not the Father but enjoyed a unique knowledge of and union with him. The words he spoke came from the Father; he did the works of God; God was in him in a way that transcended any concept known to them. He claimed that it was so and others recognized it.

The dogma of the Holy Trinity is not an abstraction, mere information regarding God's "inner life" – kind of God to give us, but quite irrelevant in our earthly existence. No! It is a stunning, blissful *experience* and is our experience, too, whether we attend to it or not. The God who created us is the God who came to us in Jesus Christ to take us back to his heart, and this same God, as the Spirit of the Risen Lord

is with us now. It was the actual experience
of this threefold presence of God as Creator,
Redeemer, Sanctifier, that led our spiritual forefathers, guided, as promised, by the Holy Spirit, to
infer that in some mysterious way, God is triune
in nature. The Church in her liturgy is always
holding up to our gaze the mystery of the triune
God. She holds it up like a precious jewel against
the light and turns it now this way, now that as
she celebrates her mysteries or preaches the word,
and so we may see it ever anew. Personally, I do
not speculate or try in any way to "work it out". I
engage in the Liturgy, I ponder scripture passages
in Paul and in John, particularly in Chapters 14
to 17 with their references to the mysterious
relationship of the Father, Son and Holy Spirit.
I "know" without conceptual knowledge that
we ourselves are caught up in the Trinitarian
stream of life. Our "position" is with the Son,
the Incarnate Son, the beloved of the Father
and lover of the Father, and, in some way that is
beyond comprehension, our love, my feeble love,
is the Holy Spirit, loving, praying deep within us.

What we perceive through our contemplation of
the Paschal mystery is that, at the very heart of
being, the ground, the origin – use what word

you will – is a communion of love, an irrepressible fountain of life, beauty, love, ever communicating itself, sharing itself in all creation but in a most special way with humankind. There is really only one life and everything partakes of it, there is no thing that has its own. All life is an outflow of that divine Fountain. Whereas other creatures share it in a natural way as belongs to created being, we humans, created though we are, are "elevated" to share God's life in a truly divine way. What we must try to grasp is that God gives God's self totally to us. God has not a hidden, private life to which we have no access. A couple might run an orphanage and devote themselves utterly to their charges, sparing themselves nothing in their love and care, finding happiness in their happiness. And yet, the door on the orphanage can close and the couple enjoy their own intimate family life with their own children, a life from which the orphans are excluded. Not so with God. We are in God's heart forever. There is no God but the God who has us in his heart and who shares divine life with us.

I learn three big things from what I understand of the blessed Trinity that are wholly relevant for the way we live. I see that it is a mystery of selflessness, of mutual self-giving: the Father, we are shown, gives all he is and has to the Son; the Son gives all he has and is to the Father. The Father is Father in begetting the Son; the Son is Son in being begotten; the Spirit is the mutual love of both. We are created in God's image and I understand something of what love means, being "out of self", given to others. I glimpse something of the Servant God whom I must try to be like. I see too something of the meaning of communion: "that they may all be one; even as thou, Father, art in me, and I in thee, that they also may be in us" (John 17:21).

It is as a people that God calls us to communion with him. We see this in the history of Israel. Israel was chosen to receive God's revelation, to become his own people living according to his will and so to become a vessel carrying his grace and light to the world. Our faith holds that the Christian Church is the fulfilment of that vocation. The Holy One of Israel, Creator of all that exists, has revealed himself "in these last days" (Heb. 1:2) as a community of love, as persons in perfect unity, and has called his people to share most intimately in this divine exchange of life. "In the image of God he made them" (Gen. 1:27). This is the reality to which we must conform our lives. "Where two or three are gathered in my name, there am I in their midst" (Matt. 18:20); it is within and through the community of believers that his life flows.

We delude ourselves if we think we can be Christian in isolation. We need the Church and everything the Church can give us: her sacraments, the proclamation and exposition of the Word of God, mutual sharing of gifts and insights, mutual support both material and spiritual. None of us can stand up alone against the forces of atheism and materialism within our society. What is more, a Christian is always as one "given", committed to others, to a community.

While recognizing the supreme necessity of community and the riches to be found therein, we do not deny the difficulties involved if we are to become, not just a group of people coming together, but a communion: individual persons drinking from the same Fountain of the Spirit and, in that Spirit, becoming "one as we are one" (cf. John 17). There is a call to selfless love, to a surrender of all selfish interests for the good of all, urged, spelled out in many ways in the New

Testament: "Look out for one another's interests rather than for your own" (Phil. 2:4); "be kind and tender-hearted to one another, forgiving one another, as God has forgiven you in Christ (Eph. 4:32). The squabbles, rivalries, jealousies of parish life are part of our repertoire of comedy, smiled at, taken for granted. Seen in their true light, in the context of God's passionate, sacrificial love for us, they are a cause for tears, not laughter. "Do not grieve the Holy Spirit of God" (Eph. 4:30).

Offence is taken because the lot has fallen on Matthias instead of on me as it should have done, for I am more fitted for the office ... I have served the Church longer ...! It isn't a matter of not feeling these things, for it is natural to do so. The important thing is what do we do with the feeling? Tell others of our grievance? Make a fuss? Show Matthias the cold shoulder? Maybe we think we have a perfect right to have the hymns we want, the Liturgy celebrated just as we like. The poor pastor does his or her best to please but there *is* no pleasing people who insist on their own way. Those holding office can be arrogant, using their sacred calling as a means of expressing their own individuality regardless of the needs of the people they are appointed to serve. All of us are selfish by nature and as Christians we are called upon and given the grace to deny our egotism, to "do nothing from selfishness or conceit, but in humility count others better than yourself" (Phil. 2:3). This is to be like our loving God. Of course, it will cost and we may well be tempted to withdraw from the parish community.

The Letter to the Hebrews, magnificent as it is, is not the easiest theological treatise to read. It is addressed to a community of Christians converted from Judaism. Placed though it is in the Pauline corpus, scarcely any scholar attributes it directly to Paul. We do not know the author or the community. To my mind, this letter has contemporary relevance. As with the community addressed, ours is a situation that in many ways tests our faith and perseverance:

> I hear it said all the day long:
> "Where is your God?". (Ps. 42(41):3)

The writer of Hebrews is deeply concerned for his people: they have lost heart, are discouraged and in danger of apostasy. We might wonder if his passionate, profound "sermon" had the desired effect. The apostles and first witnesses have died, the Lord has not returned, the years of springtime excitement and enthusiasm have passed away as they must, and there appears little to support the faith of these Christians, who are under constant harassment from the Jewish community. It seems they are dissatisfied with their Christian Liturgy and are missing the beloved, age-old, splendid rites of the Temple and the familiar services of the synagogue, from which they have been expelled. Things are very flat! Our religious life is drab! Presumably it was too early for the young Church to have expanded, with suitable rites, its central liturgy: "I received from the Lord what I also delivered to you, that the Lord Jesus on the night he was betrayed took bread, and when he had given thanks, he broke it and said, 'This is my body which is for you. Do this in remembrance of me.' In the same way also the cup, after supper, saying, 'This cup is the new covenant in my blood. Do this, as often as you drink it, in remembrance of me'" (1 Cor. 11:23–25). The "breaking of bread" and "drinking the cup" in a family home would seem a poor substitute for the highly developed liturgies they had known. The preacher summons these wilting souls to a vigorous revival of faith in Jesus and his sacrificial death as the fulfilment of all the Temple could offer and everything that was life giving and splendid in the First Dispensation.

Don't we find, at least at times, that spirituality is a dull business, that our liturgies are uninspiring and are we not in danger of slipping into apathy? This is when we must persevere, seek support from one another: "Let us hold fast the confession of our hope without wavering, for he who promised is faithful; and let us consider how to stir up one another to love and good works, not neglecting to meet together, as is the habit of some, but encouraging one another" (Heb. 10:23–25). Let us take care that we ourselves do not become a "root of bitterness", contaminating a whole community with our disgruntlement, but rather let us "strive for peace with all men, and for the holiness without which no one can see the Lord" (cf. Heb. 10:23–25; 12:15).

We would never end if we were to quote all the counsels for true Christian living, strewn throughout the Letters of the New Testament. We hear them proclaimed in our liturgies, but do they go in one ear and out the other? Do we pause, take time to examine ourselves in their

light? How we would benefit if we took just one
list, 1 Cor. 13, for instance, and seriously held up
against it our thoughts, conduct and attitudes,
and then, acknowledging our sins, expose them
to the love of Jesus and pray for the love we lack!
With these ancestors of our faith, we must keep
"looking to Jesus the pioneer and perfecter of
our faith, who for the joy that was set before him
endured the cross, despising the shame, and is
seated at the right hand of God" (Heb. 1:2). And
let us never stop striving for that selfless, unconditional, untiring, enduring love for one another
that marks us out as the true disciples of him who
gave his life for us all.

There is a ruling insight that covers and controls
my life and all that I would or could communicate to others. It runs through everything I
have written: God offers himself in total love to
each one of us. Our part is to open our hearts to
receive this gift. To use the image of a saint who
lived out this truth, God is an ocean of merciful
love that is pent up, longing to be released, to
pour itself into each one of us, but human pride,
lack of faith and trust, thrust up barriers against
it. We find it so difficult to take Jesus at his word:
that he alone is Saviour. We think we must first

save ourselves, perfect ourselves and then offer ourselves to Love. No! Only Love can save, purify, and cause us to expand and expand to receive more and more. This we learn from Jesus, for, as Julian of Norwich clearly perceived, where Jesus is there is the Trinity. In the following pages, I want to share my understanding of what it means to have been given Jesus as "our wisdom, our righteousness and sanctification and redemption" (1 Cor. 1:30), and our "Way, Truth and Life" (cf. John 14:5). All is done for us, all is given.

THREE

The World Knew Him Not

The Lord God called to the man, and
    said to him,
"Where are you?"
And he said, "I heard the sound of you
    in the garden,
and I was afraid because I was naked, and
    so I hid myself."
He said, "Who told you that you were
    naked?" (Gen. 3:9–11)

Down the long centuries, men and women have struggled with the inescapable facts of sin and evil. St Paul speaks of the "mystery of iniquity" and a mystery it remains. Don't we all ask questions, sometimes with deep anxiety: why suffering, why so much evil, how can there be a good, all-powerful God? In our day, the presence of overwhelming suffering in the world is the biggest obstacle to faith. No clear, irrefutable answer can be given this side of the grave, but some things can be said, for faith seeks understanding. A distinction must be made between sin and evil. Sin is exclusively an act of the will, whereas evil is everything that militates against human welfare and happiness. There are many evils that cannot be attributed, at least directly, to a human act. Scripture raises the question: whose will is involved in sin and evil? Are we to believe that there is another or other wills operative in the world beside the human – that of the "Adversary", as St Paul designates the agent of all that opposes the designs of God? There was a time when I dismissed the idea of a "personal" devil or Satan, and interpreted the bible's "dominations and powers", "powers of darkness" and "the prince of this world" as the seemingly uncontrollable forces or energies generated by collective wrong doing, mere errors, or the dark phantoms of the human psyche, leading to the creation of harmful structures in society, and fostering false values and objectives. These, in turn, create an environment in which it is difficult for men and women to recognize, let alone avoid, sin. Now I am not so arrogantly sure.

The angels continue to hold their place in our liturgies, and who would presume to assert that there were no other intelligent, "personal" beings beside us? Is there truth behind the Jewish myth of the fall of angels through the sin of pride? "I saw Satan falling like lightning from heaven" (Luke 10:18), Jesus declares, when his disciples return exulting in the success of their first mission, thrilled with the idea of devils being subject to them. Is this saying of Jesus a reference to that myth, and is he warning his disciples against the pride that brought down "Lucifer", the Satan? It is true that they are endowed with great authority but that is no cause for self-congratulation and rejoicing. Their only joy must lie in the security of their names being "written in heaven"; in other words, their value lies in the heart of God. Ultimately, this is the only true, lasting joy for every one of us. It is significant

that this declaration of Jesus is within the same
context as the text found in Luke and Matthew:
"In that same hour he rejoiced in the Holy Spirit
... 'All things have been delivered to me by my
Father; and no one knows who the Son is except
the Father, or who the Father is except the Son
and anyone to whom the Son chooses to reveal
him'" (Luke 10:22; Matt. 11:27).

Almost universal is the implicit if not explicit
sense that the world is not as it was meant to
be, we ourselves are not as we were meant to be.
Something has gone very wrong. Does not this
innate, maybe irrational notion persist alongside
our knowledge of an evolving universe? As
believers we confidently affirm that the original
plan of the Creator has indeed been upset: "an
enemy has done this" (Matt. 13:28). Who is the
enemy?

St Paul insists that "all have sinned and fall short
of the glory of God" (Rom. 3:23). "The glory
of God", what is it? To my mind it is the simul-
taneous showing forth of who and what God
is, and its human recognition and response in
praise and thanksgiving. In Jesus Christ, God is
revealed as absolute, unconditional, self-emptying,

self-giving love. Every one of us has fallen and still falls short of really believing in this God in such a way that we entrust our lives to him in grateful love. Applicable to each of us, at least at times, is Paul's indictment: "They exchanged the truth about God for a lie and worshipped and served the creature rather than the Creator who is blessed for ever" (Rom. 1:25).

If we turn from St Paul to the gospel according to John we find a similar line of thought. Jesus' patient effort to win over the Pharisees has, in the case of many, met with failure. The debate becomes acrimonious and the point is reached where Jesus discerns in his adversaries a deliberate rejection of the truth. They claim God as their father; Jesus responds to their claim: "If God were your father you would love me" (John 8:42). Why do they refuse? He supplies the answer: "Because you cannot bear to hear my word. You are of your father the devil, and your will is to do your father's desires. He was a murderer from the beginning, and has nothing to do with the truth, because there is no truth in him. When he lies, he speaks according to his own nature, for he is a liar and the father of lies" (John 8:42–44). This unequivocal condemnation of the devil or Satan as the primal source of murder and of lie – "from the beginning" – directs my thoughts to the story of the fall in the book of Genesis.

The author of Genesis is trying to answer our questions, the huge, ever recurring questions: why is the world as it is? Why so much suffering? Why so much sin? We must take a careful look at the story. The first man and woman are living happily in the garden the Lord has prepared for them. They take for granted that they are loved, cared for and completely safe and they enjoy a sweet intimacy between themselves and with the Lord. Then along comes the tempter and approaches the woman. We are meant to see her contemplating the tree of good and evil, the fruit of which they are forbidden to eat. Satan feigns an innocent question: "Did God say, 'You shall not eat of any tree in the garden?'" The woman assures him that is not the case: they can eat of every tree in the garden; there is just one they must leave alone, not even touch, still less eat its fruit, because it would be harmful for them, they would die; a simple, trusting reply. Then the cunning "father of lies", the "murderer from the beginning", utters the terrible, destructive lie, wholly distorting the truth of God: "You will not

47

die! God knows that when you eat of it your eyes will be opened and you will be like God, knowing good and evil." Doubt, suspicion take root in the woman's mind and heart: God is not so loving after all; he can't be relied on to do what is best for her husband and herself. He is despotic, jealous of his power and determined to keep it to himself; they are to remain under his control as if they were children. Eve, "mother of all the living", allies herself with the "father of lies". Adam, the "father of all mankind", does likewise.

Is not the inspired writer's fundamental explanation of the world's tragedy of sin and misery *a distorted image of God*, passed on from generation to generation down the long centuries? "I knew you to be a hard man, reaping where you did not sow, and gathering where you did not winnow; so I was afraid, and I went and hid your talent in the ground. Here you have what is yours" (Matt. 25:24–25).

"Lo, these many years I have served you, and I never disobeyed your command; yet you never gave me a kid, that I might make merry with my friends" (Luke 15:29). And the answer? "My son, you are always with me, and all that is mine is yours" (ibid. 31). Would that we could but glimpse, even for a moment, the utter lavishness, the excess of God's love! As it is, the loving face of the Creator is replaced by an idol, a creature fashioned from human fears and suspicions, from limitations that make men and women mistrustful, envious and jealous of one another, even to the point of wanting to be rid of the other, hence to murder. The Eden of loving harmony is lost to us. We humans have clanged shut the gates and, to a great extent, keep them shut.

It is worth noting that there is nothing in the story of Genesis to support the idea that every human being born into this world inherits, through the generative act, the stain or guilt of the sin of Adam and Eve. It is St Paul alone who is responsible for this exegesis of Genesis 3 and his purpose is simply to illustrate the universality of redemption for all who put their faith in Christ, the new Adam, be they gentile or Jew, freedman or slave: "Then as one man's trespass led to condemnation for all men, so one man's act of righteousness leads to acquittal and life for all men. For as by one man's disobedience many were made sinners, so by one man's obedience many will be made righteous" (Rom. 5:18–19).

49

In the biblical narrative, the individual person is still free to choose good or evil, although sin "crouches at the door" of every human heart as it crouched at Cain's door. Cain chose to let it in and murdered his brother, Abel. Undoubtedly, sin abounded in the world but the possibility of holiness was always there: "Enoch walked with God; and he was not, for God took him" (Gen. 5:24). This mysterious statement implies holiness. Noah and others too "found favour with the Lord" (Gen. 6:8).

The more I reflect, the more it seems to me that all sin ultimately derives from the falsehood that contorted and still contorts the true face of God. Even though we ourselves sincerely affirm our belief in the reality of God our Creator and of God as the Father of Jesus, do we consistently live in the truth that our faith affirms? Is our trust in his love constant and consistent; do we never yield to doubt in his loving care? Are there not instances, perhaps many, where we leave God aside and consult only ourselves as to what is for our good, and that is likely to be what, here and now, we want. When faced with a moral demand that, if obeyed, would seem to humiliate or diminish us in some way, can we say yes by surrendering ourselves to the steadfast love of God, which, as we know, is always intent on our good? In times of distress, darkness, turmoil, can we still perceive that loving face or do we wail: "What have I done that God should do this to me? How can God do this?" All our selfish choices derive from lack of trust in God's love and care for us. *We* know what is good for us, we know what is bad for us, or so we imagine. We simply cannot abandon ourselves in total trust because we are not looking at the true God but at an idol created by our fears, our sensuality and pride.

We exchange God's truth for a lie. We may not see this very clearly but, if we really, fully grasped "how much, how sweetly and how tenderly our Maker loveth us,"[6] we would drop our self-concern and anxious self-protectiveness. The lie lies deep within us, telling us that we have a rival in our Maker, jealous, ready to thwart our full human development and begrudging us the pleasures and happiness that this world offers. Can we gainsay St Paul as he insists: "All have sinned and fall short of the glory of God", and John the Elder: "If we say we have no sin we deceive ourselves and the truth is not in us" (1 John 1:8). What deeper prayer can we pray than:

"Show me your Face; your Face do I seek" (cf. Ps. 27(26):8–9)? Seek, seek his Face and you will find, you will come to see the truth and find freedom from all fear.

"From the beginning" our Creator and Lover has striven to communicate himself to human beings. Historical facts and present experience show that "in many and various ways" (Heb. 1:1) unknown to us, something of the truth of God has been revealed throughout the world. Nevertheless, divine Wisdom, Word, Love, chose a particular people in which to abide in a special way so that through this chosen people, knowledge of him would spread to every race on earth: "All the ends of the earth would see the salvation of our God" (Ps. 98(97):3). The Bible records the "fate" of the divine Word seeking a home with the "children of men". "He was in the world, and the world was made through him, yet the world knew him not. He came to his own home, and his own received him not" (John 1:10–11).

The Creator Spirit, always at work in the world and in human hearts, never contravenes their innate structure but works from within; not doing for men and women what they can do for themselves. True to their nature, for human nature is naturally religious, the Hebrew people sought for their God, sought for the face that, although they knew it not, was seeking them. Alas, their myopic vision as often as not perceived a hideous caricature, wrathful, vindictive, jealous for its honour. Although the Lord was knocking at the door, looking through the lattice, his face alight with love, longing to be welcomed (Song 2:9), poor, self-concerned, frightened men and women, projecting on to him their fear, their hate and anger, shut their doors and lattices.

Inexplicable, destructive natural phenomena inevitably aroused fear in primitive people and, of course, they attributed them to some wrathful deity. Dreaded too was the cruelty of powerful, rapacious foes. What they were wanting was a warrior god who would gird on his buckler and shield, and raise his mighty sword arm to crush their enemies. Through their great leader, Moses, they had learned that a God had chosen them to be his own people and had rescued them from slavery. It is the same God, so they were told, who had been worshipped by their father Abraham and was now to be known as the God of Israel. They must be loyal to him, worship him alone and have nothing to do with other gods.

Not until the exile did monotheism take hold and the prophet of the exile, Second Isaiah, was the first to give it unequivocal expression. Chapters 40 to 43, especially, are a verbal elimination of nature gods and of polytheism in general. It is hard for us to appreciate how great a spiritual achievement this was in a culture totally polytheistic. Even so, people quickly drifted back into idolatry. Utterly dependent on their harvest, subject to frequent draughts and the danger of famine, they rushed back to their fertility rites hoping thereby to placate the gods that sent rain in season, ensured fertility of human and beast. They had no illusions about the morality of their gods. Pagan gods shared the vices of humans and were basically self-seeking, caring nothing for their worshippers, and yet generations of ancestors had had nothing else to rely on. Conveniently, these gods, having no morals themselves, made no moral demands on their clients.

Unfamiliar, strange and seemingly ineffectual, Israel's God did not fit the pattern. As yet they could not know how deeply he cared and how vulnerable he was in his love. Love made stern demands that served their truest interest; to ignore them spelled disaster. However, to their way of thinking, the one supposed to be their God was shown to be powerless, unable – or unwilling – to take care of them. He did not go out with their armies to ensure their victory but let them be defeated!

He was indeed a hidden God. They saw the long, successful reign of David and Solomon as the golden age and blithely assumed that what God wanted for his people was what they wanted: a return of that golden age, when Israel would once again be a strong, independent people under its own king, taking its proud place among the nations. They were sadly mistaken:

> My thoughts are not your thoughts,
> Neither are your ways my ways, says the
> Lord.
> For as the heavens are higher than the
> earth,
> So are my ways higher than your ways
> And my thoughts higher than your
> thoughts. (Is. 55:8–9)

As revelation develops, we shall see this reversal of human values constantly repeated. In carrying out his inconceivably wonderful, blissful design for all humankind and the whole of creation, the Creator, from the quasi-infinitude of the cosmos, selects one tiny, insignificant planet to be a home of incredible beauty for his human creatures. When he comes to earth as one of us, he chooses for his earthly dwelling, not splendid Greece or Rome, but Palestine, a vulnerable coastal strip, and not its capital, Jerusalem, but Nazareth, an insignificant village, and the home of a little nobody, a virgin named Mary.

The Bible is a monumental drama of good and evil, light and darkness; every human passion is displayed and every human sin. Divine Love wandered unrecognized, unsheltered among the children of men, crying out: "Where are you?" (Gen. 3:9):

> He had no form or comeliness that we
>   should look at him,
> and no beauty that we should desire him.
> He was despised, rejected ...
> and we esteemed him not ...

Surely he has borne our griefs
and carried our sorrows. (cf. Is. 53–54)

Even in the most barbaric times, when unspeakable
cruelties were perpetrated in the name of the
God of Israel, there were those who "received
him". With Christian eyes, we look for the face
of Christ, with Christian ears, listen for his voice.
The simple, Christ-like virtues of loyalty, sacrifice,
kindness and love shine out in the Book of Ruth,
contemporaneous with the Book of Judges which
is, as much as anything, a chronicle of human sin.
We hear something of the heartbroken cry of our
Saviour in David's lament for the son who had
wronged him in every conceivable way: "Would
I had died instead of you" (2 Sam. 18:33). But
we do not recognize him in the David who
shed no tears for and ignored the desolation of
his virgin daughter, Tamar, treacherously, cruelly
raped by her half-brother, Amnon, David's son
(2 Sam.13).

In the great drama of the beginnings of divine
revelation, our attention is largely focused on the
principals, the leaders of the nation: Abraham,
Jacob, Moses, Joshua, David, who, politically,
ostensibly, carry it forward down the centuries,

but it is the people as a whole who are bearers of the Word. We do well to reflect on some minor characters whose virtue, we may assume, was representative of many others unknown to us, who acted justly, loved tenderly and walked humbly with their God (cf. Mic. 6:8). The dark chronicle of Judges reveals the depravity into which the Israelites were sinking, ending as it does with the most shocking of the many crimes the Bible records. Yet a diamond gleams in this darkness: an unnamed, unsung, forgotten heroine, a lamb of sacrifice: the daughter of Jephthah. As in the story of Abraham and his son Isaac, it is the God of Abraham who becomes the God of Israel, who supposedly demands the sacrifice of the son and daughter. Was there a greater lie than this, a greater contortion of the God of love? Abraham's upraised knife was stayed: Jephthah's knife was not.

We are not told that Isaac consented to be a victim; we know the virgin of Gilead did. The father's thought is all for himself, not for his daughter, and in chilling egotism he blames her for *his* misfortune: "Alas, my daughter, you have brought me very low, and you have become the cause of great trouble to me; for I have opened my mouth to the Lord and I cannot take back my vow." His daughter's concern is for him whom she will still call father: "My father, if you have opened your mouth to the Lord, do to me according to what has gone from your mouth." All she asked for herself was to spend two months in the mountains with her maidens, bewailing her virginity. As a sterile virgin, her life was meaningless and, it seems that the sacrifice of fruitfulness was more to her than death. True to her word, at the appointed hour, she returned, a meek lamb to slaughter (Judges 11:34ff). "Let it be to me according to your word" (Luke 1:38).

We recognize in Jonathan's pure, unselfish love for David a love such as Jesus enjoined on his disciples. Against a background of jealousy, feuds and murderous thoughts, he sacrifices every advantage to himself, everything he has to ensure David's welfare and advancement: his own position, his father's esteem and love and the presence of David himself.

Yes, they were always there, a throng of the "poor in spirit", the "meek", those who "longed for justice" and placed their trust in the Lord:

> a people humble and lowly, who seek
>   refuge in the name of the Lord …
> who do no wrong and utter no lies,
> nor shall there be found in their mouth a
>   deceitful tongue (cf. Zeph. 3:12, 13).

Without face or name, they stream down the years as a river of grace towards the "fullness of time".

FOUR

My Word is as Fire

Run, fainthearted, here are the burning
    men,
oh quickly, into the caves! If they come near
You will break uncontrollably into a fury
    of flame
that is God, that is love,
oh, they are the men to fear.

And stop your ears, cower! These wild voices
cry: God! God! Love! – and once they
    are heard,
you too become nothing but voice,
you are smelted
into a resonance sounding only the Word.

Only down in the dark, the thick warm
    moisture
are you safe, for now God is let loose.
He has seized upon men who come near
he is totally present.
Oh now, terrible joy, now is Love
    without truce.[7]

"He has spoken through the prophets." From time immemorial, men and women, conscious of their frailty and vulnerability in a mysterious, often threatening world, have longed for reassurance, longed for what would afford some sense of security. If they could be given even a glimpse of what lay ahead, they might avoid danger and even, perhaps, discern the path to good fortune. Fearfully aware of peril from every side, they sought out members of the community who gave proof of more than ordinary insight and who seemed to be endowed with magical powers which put them in touch with the unseen forces of the world: magicians, soothsayers, witch doctors, priests and prophets.

The Creator, Israel's God, made use of this natural and cultural institution for his own purpose. Just as no pagan king or tribal chief would go into battle or engage in any important business without his prophet, so it was with the kings of Israel and Judah, for example, King David had at hand his prophet, Nathan, ready to advise, warn and rebuke, and other instances could be cited (1 Kings 21:17).

With the dramatic experience of Elijah on Mount Horeb, the form of prophecy, or divine communication, undergoes a marked change. Elijah has fled far in panic from the wrath of Jezebel, and reaching Horeb, the mountain of vision, takes refuge in a cave. Was he hoping for a theophany such as Moses received? If so, he was not disappointed. Phenomena of a kind that, throughout the history of the people, had marked the presence of the Lord: devastating wind, earthquake, fire; these crashed around Elijah. Yet, contrary to expectation, the Lord was not to be recognized in this display of violence, but rather in something strange, awesome in its gentleness: "a still, small voice" or "the whisper of a gentle breeze" (no one seems sure of the exact meaning of the Hebrew word). Instinctively, Elijah discerns the divine presence: "He shall not cry out or make his voice heard in the street" (Is. 42:2; Matt. 12:19, 20).

The Lord was not in the wind, the fire, or the earthquake. Had he ever been in them, we wonder. It is hard to know how faith of any degree could have been aroused, still less have taken root, no matter how tenuous, without compelling miracles of nature. Such things impressed on the mind the awful power and majesty of God, showing him as a God to be feared, a God with whom it was dangerous to trifle.

The struggle for monotheism meant a refusal to attribute power over the world to anyone but the Lord God of Israel. It was assumed that other gods existed but none was equal to the Lord. Two hundred years or more must elapse before Second Isaiah could proclaim with joyful, triumphant certainty the one sole God, Creator of heaven and earth, a God of infinite power, majesty, compassion and beauty.

The struggle for this pure faith extends far back in time. Whatever had been God's way in the past, from now on it is through the frail, uncertain medium of the human mind and verbal utterance that he will reveal himself, and this is a persisting challenge to faith. After all, blazing mountains, earthquakes to order, carry their own authenticity. The senses are satisfied: "Yes, yes, the Lord is God!"

How are we to believe him to be present and speaking in a human voice? There is no alternative: either we reject faith altogether or attend with eager, trusting hearts to the revelation of God in ways that our human pride and our passion for proofs could never have foreseen. "Unless you see signs and wonders you will not believe" (John 4:48). "The Pharisees came and began to argue with him, seeking from him a sign from heaven, to test him. And he sighed deeply in his spirit and said, 'Why does this generation seek a sign? Truly I say to you, no sign shall be given to this generation'" (Mark 8:11–12). True faith is soldered on to the living God alone, it relies not on signs and wonders, but on God's utter fidelity. The Bible speaks of God's truth, his reliability and steadfastness; the intent of his heart remains unchanged, an absolute intent to give himself to us completely for our perfect fulfilment.

The term "literary prophets" is usually reserved for the individuals whose preaching and oracles are recorded under their name: Amos, Isaiah, Jeremiah ... but, in fact, it includes many others who, under God, were responsible for the books of the Bible as we have them today. Under God, these prophets shaped the religion of Israel. Their work extends over several centuries, during the exile, after the exile, to the second century BC. These dedicated people: scribes, priests, Temple singers, true worshippers of the living God, gathered up whatever written material had been preserved: tribal legends, ancient chronicles, the book of the Law. They worked it over, inter-preting it in the light of subsequent events. All these data were prayerfully treasured and formed part of Israel's liturgical worship, undergoing a reshaping, and amplification in the process. Compilers, preachers, translators, redactors, these people prayed, listened to God and interpreted his will. Rightly do we use the word "inspired" for the sacred book they gave to us.

In what way are we to understand the Hebrew Scriptures as the inspired word of God? It seems to me that we may not shirk this question. Our treasure, what matters most in life, far from being obvious, is hidden. A quality of mind and heart is necessary to recognize it. The gleam of its presence can be obscured by its setting, as a pearl buried under merchandise. It is my conviction that the written words are not themselves revelation but that they contain it as the field holds the treasure. The treasure has to be unearthed. It would be nearer the truth to say that the words are the human reflection on revelation and, inevitably, the interpreter's inescapable historical situation with all its implications, affects the interpretation and form of expressing it. "Truly you are a hidden God!" (Is. 45:15). How can we attribute the savagery of ethnic cleansing to the direct will of the Lord God: "Do not spare them, but kill both man and woman,

infant and suckling, ox and sheep, camel and ass"
(1 Sam. 15:3)? The cry for vengeance on enemies,
sparing neither man, woman nor child, runs down
the centuries. In no way can we accept that "this is
the word of the Lord". No, it is the word of man
at a particular period of human history.

Our absolute authority for interpreting all the
scriptures is Christ and this supremely because "it
is they that bear witness to me" (John 5:39); "and
beginning with Moses and all the prophets, he
interpreted to them in all the scriptures the things
concerning himself" (Luke 24:27). It is impossible
to know the full significance of Jesus the Christ if
we divorce him from the Old Testament. Anyone
familiar with the Church's Liturgy, especially the
liturgical celebration of the "Paschal mystery",
needs no further proof of this statement. Jesus
himself revered the Hebrew Scripture. "I have
not come to destroy but to fulfil" (Matt. 5:17).
However, he did not attribute everything in it to his
Father, on the contrary, he was ready to question
its authority. Jesus does not say: "You have heard
that it was said by your Father", rather: "It was
said to you of old"; "Moses said to you". He does
not attribute words to God his Father that are
alien to the Spirit of the Father: "You have heard

that it was said, 'You shall love your neighbour and hate your enemy.' But I say to you, Love your enemies and pray for those who persecute you" (Matt. 5:44–45). The fine dictum of Archbishop Michael Ramsey is a splendid yardstick of interpretation: "There is nothing unChristlike in God." If we bear that in mind as we immerse ourselves in the Hebrew Scriptures, we can't go wrong, or so it seems to me.

Who can remain unmoved by the writings of the prophets: those of the eighth century BC, when Israel and Judah trembled before the growing might of Assyria: Amos, First Isaiah, Hosea, to name the most well known, and later, Jeremiah and Ezekiel who prophesied when the dark shadow of Babylon lay over Judah. The Northern Kingdom had already ceased to exist and vulnerable Judah was exposed to its might. Jeremiah and his younger contemporary, Ezekiel, witnessed the horrors of the city and nation's destruction and the deportation of Judah's leading citizens. The younger man, together with the prophet, Second Isaiah, shared the lot of the exiles and prophesied their return to their homeland.

They are, indeed, burning men, rising up like fire,

men on whom the great and holy God has mysteriously laid hold. Who can doubt it? They did not:
"Thus says the Lord." It was not their choice to
prophesy, to defy the powers of the land. They
were seized upon, maybe writhing in the Lord's
grasp, but yielding at last. Everything was asked of
them: the ordinary joys and comforts of life, the
support of a community's acceptance, security.

From the start they were marked men, open to
persecution, torture and the sentence of death.
"Which of the prophets did not your fathers
persecute? And they killed those who announced
beforehand the coming of the Righteous One,
whom you have now betrayed and murdered" (Acts
7:52). They had no Jesus, no human face of God
and, moreover, no certain hope of eternal reward.
What was their experience? Awe, fear certainly;
love? However we express it, undoubtedly these
individuals knew a profound, intimate relationship
with the Lord. Love is not a feeling. Love is
"knowing the Lord" and this was consistently
understood by the prophets to mean acting as God
would wish, in other words, obeying the law:

The fool has said in his heart,
there is no God. (Ps. 14(13):1; 53(52):1)

The "fool" has not indulged in philosophical thinking and concluded that God does not exist. It is unlikely that he has thought at all beyond what here and now will satisfy his greed. The "fool" is the immoral man who flouts the commands of God. "If anyone says, 'I love God,' and hates his brother, he is a liar; for he who does not love his brother whom he has seen cannot love God whom he has not seen" (1 John 4:20).

These religious forefathers of ours had a clear realization that protestations of devotion to the Lord were worthless without obedience to the basic commandments. Sacrifices, holocausts, cultic worship were an abomination to the Lord when offered by liars, the fraudulent, murderers and adulterers. Although they inveighed against idolatry with all their might, still greater was their condemnation of the exploitation of the poor by the rich and powerful and the prevailing moral corruption. We are reminded of St Paul's indictment of society in the first chapters of Romans. Can we fail to see in what we read, a picture of our own society?

It was the bitter lot of the prophets to experience in their own heart and flesh both God's detestation of his people's apostasy and his frustrated love, and at the same time, to harbour a passionate concern for the welfare of the people, their own people, hurtling to disaster. Prophets were men torn apart. This is particularly evident in Jeremiah. Of all the prophets, he is the one we can really know. Like Samuel and the boy Jesus, he became aware of his prophetic vocation at 12 years of age. It was as a young man of 18 that he delivered the sermon in the Temple court that provoked the wrath of all who heard it. In it, he denounced the hypocrisy of Temple worship, the injustices and corruption of society. From this time on he was never free from persecution. He moaned, complained, rebelled and came to close to apostasy so enormous were the pressures under which he laboured. The Lord was unsparing of his servant. Jeremiah's complaining to the Lord of the greatness of his sufferings received cold comfort – hard is it? It is going to get much worse! However, there was always the one assurance: "I will be with you."

False prophets haunting the court were a thorn in Jeremiah's side. In his loneliness, he saw them having a good time, enjoying the favour of king and court as in the Lord's name they predicted what they wanted to happen: Babylon itself would be defeated, Judah left in safety. Poor Jeremiah thundered against these quacks: Judah was doomed. In his own person, he reflected this doom: he was forbidden to marry and beget offspring. Celibacy was unknown in Israel; a man and woman lived on only in their offspring and to die without descendants was to disappear as if one had never existed.

The cruellest of all Jeremiah's afflictions was the sense that the Lord had let him down, had called him to be his prophet, told him what he was to proclaim in his name, and yet the predictions had not come true. Events seemed to vindicate the optimistic prophets. This was gall! Jeremiah was, indeed, a disillusioned young man with a deep grudge against the Lord who had deceived him. In his bitterness, he came close to cursing God and turned away from him, but repented when the Lord assured him that all was not lost, he would be welcomed back into his service.

In the eighth century, Isaiah, at the Lord's command, forbade the king of Judah to seek security through alliances with powerful neighbours. Judah must trust in the Lord alone – no

easy thing to do when danger is approaching!
More galling still, he was to submit to the
Assyrian yoke, accepting to be a vassal and Judah
a conquered people. Similarly, it was Jeremiah's
bitter, dangerous mission, not merely to prophesy
certain defeat, but to insist on submission to
Babylon. It was the Lord's will, he declared,
that Nebuchadnezzar should rule the world
for a period of time. These predictions and
commands completely undermined national
religious securities. Was not Judah the Lord's
chosen kingdom, irrevocably established by his
sworn promise? Had not the Lord's own people
been guaranteed possession of the land forever,
with a king of David's line upon the throne?
Why, Jerusalem was the pole of the earth and its
temple the Lord's earthly dwelling and what was
Jeremiah but a dangerous madman who should
be eliminated?

So intense was the desire of the king and the
powerful of the land for Judah to be once again
a great nation that, in spite of all warnings, they
seized every opportunity to rebel. Each attempt
to be great was thwarted. God's desire was for
Israel to be small and powerless on the world's
stage. The people schemed for greatness, for an

earthly kingdom, and the Lord was offering a different kind of kingdom, one yet to come. When their lack of faith and disobedience ended in total disaster, the Lord did not abandon them. He was with the exiles in Babylon and with the pitiful remnant left behind in Judea. The passion for worldly greatness was not eradicated and would persist down the centuries into the time of Jesus.

Jeremiah and all the Lord's prophets represent a band of faithful ones who, baffled though they were by events and the seeming absence of the Lord, struggled faithfully on in bitter suffering, carrying forward for us the torch of divine revelation, men and women "of whom the world was not worthy ... And all these, though well attested by their faith, did not receive what was promised, since God had seen something better for us, that apart from us they should not be made perfect" (Heb. 11:38–40). With our Christian insight, we discern a truth that is a continual challenge to each one of us. Israel was, indeed, God's chosen people with a particular vocation, but it was for God, not for them, to decide on how that vocation should be realized. They could not see into the future and see how truly, how mysteriously, the great promises to

Israel would be fulfilled. The people of the past were asked to accept God's mysterious ways in the night of faith: "Trust me, leave yourselves in my hands." For very many, this was too hard a saying. Faced with a crisis, against God's will, they took the initiative, desperately trying to manipulate events and even God himself, refusing to believe that he was their absolute saviour and, if they would but trust him, ultimately, not a hair of their head would perish. What matter if they were conquered? What matter if they found themselves in the valley of darkness: "I will be with you", and that is all that really matters to human beings. Do we not see ourselves in these ancestors of ours?

Jesus' disciples were caught in a violent storm on the lake and were sinking, while the Lord lay peacefully sleeping. Terrified, indignant, they shook him awake, reproaching him for his indifference. There they were, desperately striving to keep from sinking and he was doing nothing, sleeping! Jesus deflates their high emotion with a reproach of his own. Why the panic? Where is your faith? Is he not saying: "Does it matter if you do go down provided I am with you?" How profound this is! "My ways are not your ways."

Are we not struggling ourselves, every day, to assimilate what the Lord was trying to teach his people long ago? Our only real need is God. We are made for God, Our destiny is in God and he created us in order to bring us to it. We persist in wanting to be god to ourselves, thinking that we know the shape of our destiny and how to reach it. Like our religious ancestors we are unable to believe that God will be God to us in every way if only we will let him. The more highly developed a people, the wider their knowledge and ability to control worldly factors, the greater the danger of illusion. To an extent that is probably unprecedented, our minds are bombarded with fascinating information that science and technology provide. Man seems supreme, he is his own lord and master, everything is lawful for him; no one has a right to tell him what is right and wrong. The ego with its opinions and wants is law unto itself. Objective truth does not exist. Seen through the eyes of faith this is a desolate landscape but it remains God's world for which Jesus died and over which the Spirit broods. As disciples of Christ in *this* historical age, our lives must proclaim: "The Lord is God!":

Son of man, say to the prince of Tyre,
    "Thus says the Lord
God:
Because your heart is proud,
and you have said, 'I am a god,
I sit in the seat of the gods,
in the heart of the seas',
yet you are but a man, and no god ..."

    ...

by your wisdom and your understanding
you have gotten wealth for yourself
and have gathered gold and silver
into your treasuries;
by your great wisdom in trade
you have increased your wealth –
and your heart has become proud in your
    wealth –
therefore thus says the Lord God:
"Because you consider yourself as wise as
    a god,
therefore, behold, I will bring strangers
    upon you,
the most terrible of the nations;
and they shall draw their swords
against the beauty of your wisdom
and defile your splendour.

They shall thrust you down into the Pit."
   (Ez. 28:1–8)

...

Son of man, raise a lamentation over the
   king of Tyre, and say to him,
"Thus says the Lord God:
You were a signet of perfection,
full of wisdom
and perfect in beauty.
You were in Eden, in the garden of God;
every precious stone was your covering

...

on the day you were created
they were prepared.

...

You were blameless in your ways
from the day you were created,
until iniquity was found in you ...
so I cast you as a profane thing from the
   mountain of God,
and the guardian cherub drove you out
from the midst of the stones of fire.
Your heart was proud because of your
   beauty." (Ez. 28:11–17)

Have this mind among yourselves which
    was in Christ Jesus,
who, though he was in the form of God,
did not count equality with God a thing
    to be grasped,
but emptied himself, taking the form of a
    servant,
being born in the likeness of men.
And being found in human form he
    humbled himself
and became obedient unto death,
even death on a cross.
Therefore God has highly exalted him
and bestowed on him the name
which is above every name,
that at the name of Jesus every knee
    should bow,
in heaven and on earth and under the
    earth,
and every tongue confess that Jesus
    Christ is Lord,
to the glory of the Father. (Phil. 2:5–11)

FIVE

The Word Became Flesh

I called on thy name, O Lord,
from the depths of the pit;
thou didst hear my plea, "Do not close
thine ear to my cry for help!"
Thou didst come near when I called on
    thee;
thou didst say, "Do not fear!"
Thou hast taken up my cause, O Lord,
thou hast redeemed my life.
    (Lam. 3:55–58)

"I will come myself and heal him." These words from the story of the healing of the centurion's son as found in Matthew, greet us at Mass on the first Monday of Advent and never fail to move me. "I will come myself. There is no question of my sending anyone else. In fact, no one else can do for you what I am going to do."

A little ceremony surrounds the solemn announcement of our Saviour's birth towards the end of our Morning Office of Christmas Eve. Although we have heard it sung year after year, I doubt if any one of us is not moved anew as the theme steadily proceeds to its climax. I will make no attempt to comment as the text speaks for itself, although the script cannot convey the musical setting with its variations of tone:

Cantor: The twenty-fifth day of
December, alleluia.

R. *Lift up your heads for your redemption is at hand.*

Cantor: In the five thousand one hundred and ninety-ninth year of the creation of the world;

From the time when God, in the
beginning, created the heaven and the
earth.

R. *Lift up your heads for your redemption
is at hand.*

Cantor: The two thousand nine hundred
and fifty-seventh year after the flood;
The two thousand and fifteenth year
from the birth of Abraham;
The one thousand and tenth year from
Moses and the going forth of the people
of Israel from Egypt.

R. *Lift up …*

Cantor: The one thousand and thirty-
second year from the anointing of David;
in the sixty-fifth week according to the
prophecy of Daniel.

R. *Lift up ….*

Cantor: In the one hundred and ninety-
fourth Olympiad; the seven hundred and

fifty-second year from the foundation of
the city of Rome,
The forty-second year of the rule of
Octavian Augustus.

R. *Lift up ...*

Cantor: All the earth being at peace,
Jesus Christ the eternal God and the son
of the eternal Father,
Willing to consecrate the world by his
holy and merciful coming,
Being conceived by the Holy Spirit, and
nine months having passed since his
conception –
Was born in Bethlehem of Judah of
the Virgin Mary, being made man. (At
this point we do not need the rubric
telling us to fall on our knees. We do it
instinctively.)

R. *The Word became flesh, alleluia,*
alleluia.

Cantor: The Nativity of Our Lord Jesus
Christ according to the flesh.

"In the fullness of time." What is the meaning of this pregnant phrase? It seems to indicate that the time was ripe for the fulfilment of God's plan for our redemption. As the centuries passed, the need for a saviour had become more and more apparent and the people yearned for him to come. When would the promises of God be fulfilled? When would "the consolation of Israel" appear, when the "redemption of Israel" (cf. Luke 2:25, 38)? Now, the time has come. Why now?

The First Dispensation with the Law and sacrificial rites has achieved its purpose to form "a people humble and lowly" who know their need of God (Zeph. 3:12). It cannot do more for them. The Holy of Holies still remains inaccessible; the joyful cry: "I see the heavens opened and the Son of Man standing at the right hand of God" (Acts 7:55) is yet to be heard.

Unknown to the world, hidden away in an obscure Galilean village, a young virgin, embodying in herself all that is purest and holiest in Judaism, has been divinely prepared to conceive and give birth to the saviour who is the Word of God. By her loving consent to God's gracious plan, on behalf of all creation she can welcome its Lord and Saviour.

The Incarnation is an event in the history of our material world and we can perceive concrete, worldly factors that demonstrate the appropriateness of the chosen moment. "When the whole world was at peace." Although this "peace" was established and enforced by military power, it proved to be a blessing not least in that Judea was protected from hostile neighbours, and if Rome imposed heavy taxation on her conquered people, provided her rule was accepted, her government had much to commend it. Rebellion she would not tolerate; it was crushed and punished it with ruthless cruelty. This relatively peaceful situation was essential for Jesus' ministry. If Israel had been under attack and war raging, Jesus could not have exercised his ministry as he did, he and his band travelling freely throughout the land. Furthermore, Rome provided a network of roads between the provinces and leading them to Rome. It was down these that the first missionaries travelled in a way that would have been inconceivable in earlier times. Strong colonies of Jews had long settled in the cities of the Empire, notably in Antioch and Rome. As with their brethren in Palestine, they were allowed freedom of worship and the protection of the State, at least in the earliest decades. These well-established, well-organized Jewish communities were to be the first mission fields of the Apostles. The more spiritual dimension of "readiness" in the world is impossible to assess but that it was a reality we can be sure. The benefits of Roman law and government may well have had their part to play in the early formation of the Christian community.

The liturgical season of Advent, Christmas and Epiphany offers many themes for our contemplation, but I find myself concentrating almost entirely on the sheer fact: *the Word was made flesh*, or the Word *became* flesh: foetus, newborn infant – no gracious words falling from his lips, no mighty deeds – silent, helpless – nothing to take our attention from the sheer *event, fact*. Here lies the Word, the divine Word who "was" from the beginning, who "was with God" and who "was God". And to add further stress: "He was in the beginning with God." We are looking down into a fathomless abyss. "Let all mortal flesh keep silence." Yet our subject is of mortal flesh, something we can talk about, something known to us.

All I can do is to try to share my own way of contemplating this mystery. It is the employment of the verb "to be" in the Prologue of John that holds my attention. We are meant to notice the sharp contrast between "was", understood as "ever was of its own self ", and "was made to be"; or the contrast between "being its very self" and "coming to be", "being made to be". Only the Word "was". All else, everything whatsoever, "becomes" or "was made", and all "through him, and without him was not anything made that was made". And, incredible though it seems, this Word, this unmade Word through whom everything was made, *becomes made*.

We are saying that the Word, which is the self-expression of God and therefore God, actually *becomes* something other than he is, becomes a made thing, a creature. Put in another way, God becomes something he was not before, acquires a new form of existence, a new experience, namely, that of being human, flawed as we are, from conception to death, in this world as it is:

> All flesh is grass
> and all its beauty is like the flower of the
>   field.

> The grass withers, the flower fades ... (Is.
>   40:6, 7)

Only God, while remaining God, can become something other. The "becomes" is absolute. God *becomes* man – no pretence, absolute reality.

And so we return to gaze upon this tiny, fragile, helpless little creature, totally dependent on his mother for his coming into the world and for the preservation of his fragile life. Were she not to feed him, caress him, keep him warm, he would die:

> Art thou not from everlasting,
> O Lord my God, my Holy One?
> Thou dost not die. (Hab. 1:12)

Why has the all-blessed One let himself in for this! What a crazy, crazy thing for him to do! Yes, it is and the only answer is that he is "crazy" in his love:

> He was so small you could not see
> His large intent of courtesy.[8]

From now on the Eternal God-become-man is completely in our hands, for us to do with him what we wish; we can treat him with love, with indifference or hatred. In his human nature he draws on no divine power, on no divine knowledge to defend himself from malice or to attain his end. He has "emptied" himself of his divine attributes; speaking metaphorically, he left them behind on the other side of the border. The evangelist, John, gives symbolic expression to this "divesting" in order to take on the nature and function of a slave, in his account of Jesus' last supper with his disciples: "Jesus ... knowing that the Father had given all things into his hands, and that he had come from God and was going to God, rose from supper, laid aside his garments, and girded himself with a towel ... and began to wash the feet of his disciples" (John 13:3–5). He has come to be with us, to share our human existence, to heal and save us: "My people is stricken with a very grievous wound which only I can heal. True, they are wounded by the consequences of sin, but there is a deeper wound still, that only I can perceive and which they themselves scarcely recognize. It is a wound of love that I myself have inflicted, an open wound for which there is no natural healing. I myself *am* the healing of that wound, that ever-aching, unsatisfied desire." Could we conceive of

91

any greater love than is shown us here – in this conception and birth? We know it is all one with that final surrender to a cruel death:

> The haughty looks of man shall be
>   brought low,
> and the pride of man shall be humbled;
> and the Lord alone will be exalted in that
>   day. (Is. 2:11)

The angel's proclamation to the shepherds of a "great joy" has echoed down the centuries and the Christian people have employed every talent, exhausted all they have of music and song, to express their sheer delight and gratitude for the birth of their Saviour. Don't we find that a phrase, or a particular bar of music catch the heart and afford a perception, a glimpse of I know not what, "Thoughts that do often lie too deep for tears",[9] which systematic meditation or hard intellectual effort do not achieve? "Silent night, holy night … Oh what light …"!:

> We saw thee in thy balmy nest,
> Young dawn of our eternal day;
> We saw thine eyes break from their east,
> And chase the trembling shades away.

We saw thee, and we blest the sight,
We saw thee by thine own sweet light.[10]

"Great joy"; if only we could really absorb it, how
it would put everything else in perspective! This
joy is not ephemeral, not dependent on anything
but itself; it is "my" joy, Christ's own joy, which
is our absolute security, the answer to all our grief
and our eternal home.

Gazing on this tiny human being, while affirming
the reality of what we actually see, hear and feel: a
human child like any human child; a humanity as
real as our own; we must as strongly affirm what
we do not perceive with our senses: this Child
is God. Mary has brought forth a human Child
who is God. There is no commingling: divine
attributes are in no way present in this human
Child. Totally man, totally God, an impenetrable
mystery! Let all mortal flesh keep silence, in awe
and adoration, yes, but we are invited to contemplate this mystery, ponder it from this angle and
that. Impenetrable it remains for our joy. How
dreadful it would be so to rationalize what we
see, and the information we are given, of God in
human form, treating it as if it were a scientific
puzzle capable of solution if only we could find

the key! Whatever we can grasp with our minds cannot be God. To grasp something means that we possess it, control it, that it is less than us. Such acquisitions can never satisfy the human spirit that is made for the infinite. Our longing, our need is for infinite Mystery and we can be satisfied with nothing less.

The *Creator almus siderum* has become human. The cosmos itself is ultimately an impenetrable mystery. Science reveals facts that overwhelm our minds and imaginative faculties and can produce feelings of terror as well as wonder. Our existence, we ourselves are mystery and I do not see how we can be truly Christian without accepting and even rejoicing to live in mystery, knowing that all derives from and is encompassed by the one holy Mystery, whose human face it is given us to see and to recognize in it a limitless, selfless love. The preface for the Mass of Christmas acclaims the mystery of Christ's birth as a new, radiant showing forth of God, of God's true nature and God's incredible love for us.

To look upon this Child, on the man he becomes, is to see God in a human being. Everything he says and does, his very way of being, mirrors the divine form. He is the "image of the invisible God" (Col. 1:15). The goodness and kindness of God our Saviour and his love for humankind that had always been there but mostly unrecognized, is now shining out in a way we cannot misunderstand (cf. Titus 3:4). Through looking on this Jesus, learning to know him, we are drawn to love and surrender to the Mystery which we cannot see and which is yet our heart's desire. Gazing on him we know without any doubt that here is not *a* mystery, but *the* Mystery of absolute beauty, goodness and love.

An American scientist writes of how, as an adolescent, confronted with scientific accounts of nature's workings, she was plunged into despair:

> The night sky was ruined. I would never
> be able to look at it again ... A bleak
> emptiness overtook me whenever I
> thought of what was really going on out
> in the cosmos or deep in the atom. So
> I did my best not to think about such
> things ...
>
> I have come to understand that I can
> deflect the apparent pointlessness of it

all by realizing that I don't have to seek
a point. In any of it. Instead, I can see
it as the locus of Mystery ... Inherently
pointless, inherently shrouded in its own
absence of category.

The clouds passing across the face of
the deity in the stained-glass images of
Heaven ...

She comes to see that she needn't seek answers
to the Big Questions and she finds peace in
acceptance. Acceptance serves her "as an epiphany
... Mystery generates wonder, and wonder
generates awe. The gasp can terrify or the gasp
can emancipate."[11]

The divine Word in becoming human has become
a part of the cosmos. He is our "locus of Mystery".
His humanity derives from the cosmos as does
ours, is composed of that unfathomable stuff we
call matter. What a comfort this is! He comes into
the same unpredictable world as we do. Each of
us, of necessity, is born of a particular family, in a
particular geographical area, at a particular point
in history. So much of us is "given", completely
outside our control. We might be in a particular

place at a particular moment when a violent earthquake or tsunami threatens our very lives or destroys our habitation and livelihood. We might fall victim to a plague, fall a casualty of war ... there is no end to the hazards and threats in our perilous existence. God himself comes to share this vulnerability. Clearly, he knew of floods and violent winds that could sweep away house and home; he knew of earthquakes and famines and strange, threatening portents in the firmament. Over and above these natural disasters, he was fully aware of the horrors of war, of human malice and cruelty. He was fully aware of what happened when a city fell, what happened to the women and children, and the butchering that turned streets into rivers of blood. Have we ever noticed his sensitivity to pregnant and nursing mothers, making special mention of them in his prediction of Jerusalem's terrible fate? "Alas for those who are with child and for those who give suck in those days!" (Luke 21:23; Mark 11:17; 24:19); and to the women who bewalled and lamented him as he made his painful journey to Calvary: "Daughters of Jerusalem, weep not for me, but weep for yourselves and for your children. For behold the days are coming when they will say, 'Blessed are the barren, and the wombs that never

bore, and the breasts that never gave suck!'"
(Luke 23:28).

Yes, Jesus, the Incarnate Word, knew about these
terrible things that still go on and crush our hearts
and bewilder our minds and awaken in us deep
anxieties that assail our faith: Where, oh where is
our God? We see his compassion for every kind
of human suffering, a compassion that urged him
to relieve it whenever he could, even at the risk
to his own life. But never did human wickedness,
the brutality of masters for their slaves, and kings
for their subjects, the horrors of war or natural
disasters, shake his fundamental serenity: "Your
Father knows." John gives full expression to this
great trust and serenity in Jesus' words to his
disciples before the terrible night of his passion
and death engulfed them. "Let not your heart be
troubled, no matter what it looks like, no matter
how hopeless everything seems, no matter how
black the night. Do not lose faith and trust in
God and in me. You will see me broken, defeated,
tortured beyond human semblance, but do not
lose trust, do not fear" (cf. John 14:1).

As Christians, we must try to overcome timidity
and fear as science progresses and seems to raise

frightening possibilities, and even threatens to undermine our faith in God. Our only answer, but a rock-safe one, is Jesus. God himself has become part of the world he made, and still maintains in existence. Christ is the beginning, the meaning and the end of the cosmos, of all that is. He alone has the absolute authority to say: "Fear not! Fear not!" "I have overcome the world" (John 16:33).

It is essential for us, if we would be true disciples, to study the gospels for ourselves and not to rely wholly on others' interpretation. We have to allow ourselves to be confronted with Jesus and learn to penetrate and absorb his words, bearing in mind the question: what is this telling me about God, for where Christ is there is the Trinity, as Julian of Norwich affirmed. I think some of us – and I certainly – have been bewildered by the way the Trinitarian nature of God is expressed. In the New Testament letters, God, Christ and Spirit are used with the implicit assumption that no one would think in terms of three gods! It is the use of "person" that confuses us as, automatically, person implies an individual that, by its very nature, is separated from every other individual. "God so loved the world that he gave his only

Son" (John 3:16). Paul: "God did not spare his own Son but gave him up for us all" (Romans 8:32). The impression made is that there is a God, out there, uninvolved, who sends his Son who likewise is God, to bear the brunt of it all. This is a false impression. There is no uninvolved divine Person: "The whole Trinity wrought in the passion of Christ." God himself, none other, comes down to us to be with us in the "pit" in order to take us up to "be with me where I am" (John 17:24) and for ever. God gives his entire Self, holding nothing back, nothing whatsoever. His love for us is absolute. It falls to us to fix our minds and hearts on the Gift of God that is Jesus Christ our Lord, to make him the lodestar of our lives.

SIX

He Lived Among Us

"Comfort, comfort my people",
says your God.
"Speak tenderly to Jerusalem,
and cry to her
that her warfare is ended,
that her iniquity is pardoned." (Is. 40.1)

Five centuries have passed since Isaiah received this command from the Lord and still Jerusalem's cheeks are wet with tears:

> From the daughter of Sion has departed
> all her majesty. (cf. Lam.1:6)

The Lord's chosen people, for all that they dwell in the land which the Lord himself had given them, feel exiled still, waiting still to be delivered from the hands of their enemies and of all who hate them, waiting still for the forgiveness of the sins that have been their ruin. Jerusalem "that was a princess among the cities" (Lam. 1:1), now dominated and defiled by a pagan conqueror, is no longer their holy home, and "they have no prince, no prophet, no leader" (Dan. 3:38 apoc.). Herod's temple adorns and crowns the city, but many Jews, unimpressed by its grandeur, refuse to recognize it as the true Temple. Corrupt sycophants of the ruling class exploit it to their own advantage and many of the serving priests are unworthy of their office. Not a few ardent Jews have abandoned the city, gone out into the wilderness to form a highly organized community, living by a Rule they hold to be true to the Jewish heritage. Others, probably the majority, believe they can offer true worship within the temple, devoutly joining in the prayers and divinely ordained sacrificial rites, regardless of the moral state of those who officiate. Such were the family, acquaintances, disciples and followers of Jesus. Even such as these, the most devout and enlightened of Israel, still mourned the loss of:

> all the precious things
> that were hers from days of old.
> (Lam. 1:7)

The One who alone could comfort them seemed far away. No echo of his voice reached them. Sadly, they thought of days long past when the Lord held familiar intercourse with their forefathers, the patriarchs, and spoke with Moses face to face. He had sent them prophets to lead, to guide, to warn them but, alas, not only did their warnings pass unheeded but these servants of the Lord were persecuted, tortured, murdered. Now only silence, and "no one to tell us how long it will last" (Dan. ibid). The prophecy of Amos seems relentlessly true:

> I will send a famine on the land;

not a famine of bread, not a thirst for
water,
but of hearing the words of the Lord.
(Amos 8:11)

Yet the one true Comforter, the Word of God himself, living and life-giving bread by which man and woman truly live, *is* there, unrecognized, among them. The time has come when it will no longer be: "Thus says the Lord", but "I say to you". John, the son of Zechariah, that "burning and shining light" (John 5:35), the greatest and last of all the prophets, proclaims that the Messiah has come, and at a certain moment is to identify him as Jesus of Nazareth.

Can we imagine the excitement, the thrilling expectancy aroused by the news, spreading through town and countryside, of a man, bearing all the marks of a prophet, prophesying the advent of the Messiah and his day of judgment? His call was for repentance and the acceptance of a baptism in the Jordan as a symbol of repentance. From all parts of the country the famished people flocked to him, captivated by his appearance and his authoritative words. Willingly, they consented to be plunged in the purifying waters.

Expectancy rose high: was John himself the Messiah? John unequivocally denied it: "I am not the Messiah"; he was nothing but a voice "crying in the wilderness", urging the people to prepare for the Lord's visitation (cf. Is. 40:3). John the herald is crying out his message "in the wilderness". It is "in the wilderness" that the Lord will speak to the heart of his people, in their "famine", in their exile, in their poverty and their sense of need, not in the self-chosen, geographical wilderness of the "pure ones" (cf. Is. 41:14, 17–20).

Neither John nor his hearers can have had any notion of the magnitude of the blessings in store for them, what prophets and kings and yearning hearts of long ago had longed and longed to see, longed and longed to hear and yet had not seen, had not heard. How blessed their eyes when they see what they are to see and their ears to hear what they are to hear (cf. Luke 10:23–24). What gracious words will fall from the lips of the "fairest of the children of men" (Ps. 45(44):2)! But will they "see", will they "hear"? We can trace the lowly path the Word has travelled with his people down the centuries, adapting himself to their condition, speaking through events and through his chosen prophets, with no show of power and no false allure, in order to woo his human children through his love alone. One after another, his faithful servants, the prophets have been tortured and killed. Divine Love throws its last card: "I will send my beloved son: maybe they will respect him" (Luke 20:13). What is to be the fate of this "son", the Word made flesh, "sent" to this distressed, blind, sinful, yearning people?

John heralds the visitation of the promised one in language reminiscent of the prophets of old. "The one who is coming after me is mightier than I, whose sandals I am not worthy to carry; he will baptise you with the Holy Spirit and with fire. His winnowing fork is in his hand, and he will clear his threshing floor and gather his wheat into the granary, but the chaff he will burn with unquenchable fire" (Matt. 3:11–12). "He said therefore to the multitudes that came out to be baptised by him: 'You brood of vipers! Who warned you to flee from the wrath to come?'" (Luke 3:7). The people readily recognized this as the voice of a prophet like those the Lord had sent them in times past.

What were the people expecting? Can we surmise the shape, so to speak, of their expectation? We find it outlined in the angelic message to Mary: "He will be great; and will be called the Son of the Most High; and the Lord God will give him the throne of his ancestor David; and he will rule in the house of Jacob for ever; and of his kingdom there will be no end" (Luke 1:32–33). Such, we deduce, would be the general supposition of the faithful. The Son of the Most High, the Messiah, would usher in and maintain the kingdom in which justice and peace would abound. Then they would surely know that God had taken them back to his heart as his own people and that the new covenant, foretold by Jeremiah (31:31–34), was established, never again to be broken. Blessed, blessed hope! However, John warned the people that a fearful judgment, a baptism of fire and a winnowing must take place before all this could happen.

We know how mysteriously, in a way more wonderful than could have been foreseen, this promise was and will continue to be fulfilled until it reaches its perfect consummation. But can it surprise us that, in the historical situation, Jesus, the carpenter from Nazareth, preaching with unheard-of authority in the name of God; claiming to be "greater than the temple", "lord of the Sabbath" (Matt.12:6–8), "greater than Jonah", "greater than Solomon" (Luke 11:29–32) should, to put it mildly, disconcert his people? Simeon had prophesied that the Child he took in his arms would be "for the fall and rise of many in Israel; for a sign that shall be contradicted", and for his holy mother a sword to pierce her soul "that out of many hearts thoughts may be revealed" (Luke 2:34–35). "The word of God is living and active, sharper than any two-edged sword, piercing to the division of soul and spirit, of joints and marrow, and discerning the thoughts and intentions of the heart. And before him no creature is hidden, but all are open and laid bare to the eyes of him with whom we have to do" (Heb. 4:12–13).

It is as if the very presence of the Incarnate Word breaks open the human heart revealing its truth or falseness, testing the reality of our faith. He himself, in his truth and goodness, is the winnowing fan. Will we allow God to be God as he is or will we insist on holding to our own ideas of God and of how God should be and should act? Are we open to recognize and surrender to the God who does not fulfil our very human expectations, our inherited suppositions and prejudices, our self-centredness and the pride that wants a God who will reward us with an enhancement of our experience of life and bestow a spiritual status on us above "the rest of men"? Do we maintain a stubborn desire for a God who acts with power and puts an end here and now to the dreadful things that occur hour by hour on our planet?

When Jesus stands before Pilate and is questioned regarding his kingship, he replies: "My kingship is not of this world ... my kingship is not from the world." "So you are a king?" Pilate asks. Jesus replies: "You say that I am a king. For this I was born, and for this I have come into the world, to bear witness to the truth. Everyone who is of the truth hears my voice" (John 18:36–37). He is the embodiment of truth, Truth himself, and bearing witness by how he is, by what he says and does, to the truth about God and the truth about man. It is impossible to know what it is to be a human person without knowing the true God. Jesus is the revelation of the true God and is also *the one true* Man. In his own person, Jesus confronts and confounds the father of lies.

Battle is joined between the Son of Man and Satan the deceiver, the prince of this world, the murderer from the beginning. Everyone stands or falls according to their allegiance. Lent is a time for assessing our allegiance as best we can, allowing our hearts to be pierced by the word of God and his holy truth, and for imploring an outpouring of grace. "Ask and you will receive" (Luke 11:9).

Even the purest of creatures, Jesus' mother, daughter of Judah, had imbibed the innocent suppositions of her people. She understood that she was to conceive and bear the Messiah, but where now the proof? Her son showed no signs of being Israel's saviour; rather, she saw him heading for disaster, seemingly unable to avert his fate. How could a disgraced, crucified man be the Messiah? We know that her faith proved equal to the cruel challenge and she bowed in submission to the will of the Most High in the dark, fearful mystery of her tortured, humiliated, murdered Son. She surrendered her inherited conceptions of the Messiah. In steadfast loyalty, she stood by him in his agony and degradation: "scorned by men, despised by the people" (Ps. 22(21):6).

John the Baptist, languishing in prison, was bewildered, disappointed even, by what his disciples told him of the preaching and actions of the one he had boldly proclaimed to be the Messiah. If he were truly the Messiah, where the evidence, where the winnowing, where the baptism of fire? Why was he, his prophet, his "friend" who had rejoiced in his presence and ascendancy (cf. John 3:28–30), left at the mercy of a tyrant? Had not his whole existence up to the point of his appearing in the wilderness, been completely devoted to preparing for his vocation? In his distress, John sent messengers to Jesus with the poignant question, "Are you the one who is to come or do we have to wait for another?" (Matt. 11:3).

Jesus sends no reassuring, affirmative answer to his faithful friend. The envoys are bidden report to their master just what they see and hear – no more than what John already knows but seen now in the context of the prophecy of Isaiah: "the blind receive their sight and the lame walk, lepers are cleansed and the deaf hear and the dead are raised up, and the poor have the good news preached to them" (Matt.11:5; cf. Is. 35:5–6, 61:1). Jesus ends with a plea that is yet a challenge: "Blessed is he who takes no offence at me" (Matt. 11:6; cf. Luke 7:18–23). It was not given to this noble man to hear the glowing testimony the Lord pays to him (Matt. 11:7–11; Luke 7:24–28). John in his dark night must decide. "Blessed are those who have not seen and yet believe" (John 20:29). This is indeed the hour of judgment when many will fall and many rise. And we ourselves – will we stand or fall?

The prince of this world disguised as an angel of light deceived many devout Jews, playing into their spiritual pride and their complacency as faithful adherents of the Law, unlike "the rest of men" (Luke 18:11). Such was Saul the Pharisee, who "advanced in Judaism beyond many of my own age among my people, so extremely zealous was I for the traditions of my fathers" (Gal.1:14). This ardent defender of the God of his ancestors and his holy Law, raged with fury against the pretensions of the Nazarene, this supposed Messiah. In the grip of the father of lies, Saul was a murderer applauding the crucifixion of the "Impostor" (Matt. 27:63), complicit in the death of Stephen and out to eliminate all the adherents of the new sect. Who could have foreseen that here was God's chosen vessel who,

113

consumed with love for the Crucified, would
work with tireless zeal, endure severest sufferings
in order to spread knowledge of his beloved Lord
across the Roman Empire, to become a light to
the gentiles, those "cursed", those outside the
Law? Saul become Paul recognized the infinite
mercy shown to him the "greatest of sinners"
(1 Tim. 1:15–16), chosen before he was born
to receive to an unsurpassable extent and depth,
the revelation of the glory of God in the face of
Christ and in him crucified. He, just as truly as
the pagans, had exchanged the glory of God for
a lie and worshipped an idol until it pleased God
"to reveal his Son to me" (Gal. 1:16).

We Christians of today are heirs of this blessed
revelation. It is given to us, through no merit
of ours, to have been taken from the realm of
darkness into God's glorious light. We recognize
the glory of God shining in the face of Christ
and only there. What had been of ultimate
abhorrence to Paul, the claim that a "criminal"
hanging on a gibbet was God's Messiah, becomes
the theme of his preaching. He will not pander
to human pride. He will preach no other Christ
than the one who was crucified, "a stumbling
block to Jews and folly to Gentiles, but to

those who are called, both Jews and Greeks, Christ the power of God and the wisdom of God" (1 Cor. 1:23–24). "O the depths of the riches and wisdom and knowledge of God! How unsearchable are his judgments and how inscrutable his ways!" (Rom. 11:33). When we humbly draw close to him in his beloved Son, we perceive his ways to be beautiful and true, joy to the heart, light to the eyes, for they are the ways of perfect love.

I suggested in my Introduction that a deep understanding of what we might call the objective realities of our faith is woefully lacking. Am I correct in asserting that most of our attention and energy spreads out on the horizontal level? We are zealous for creating community, for fostering parish life, for promoting social justice whether at home or on the international level and for all works of mercy and, indeed, we cannot be truly Christians without such concerns. Yet perhaps we should ask ourselves if we are not too taken up with our own initiatives and activities, with our *own* good works, and fail somewhat in attention to the first commandment, that we must love God with our whole heart, soul, mind and strength. Unless the first commandment dominates our life and motivates our concerns, then there is danger of our just beating the air.

Our busyness on the social level could spring from subtle self-seeking and an instinct to avoid what may be a less self-satisfying orientation. As Christians, our first duty, our *glory* is to remember the deeds of the Lord and the wonderful things he has done, to stand in awe at his deeds, to give him thanks for being what he is. We have a positive obligation to reflect constantly on what Christ is to us, what he has done for us, on the absoluteness of his victory, on the marvellous riches at our disposal.

Our faith must be a rock-like certainty that God, in Christ, has given us everything, guaranteed an inheritance that cannot be spoiled and can never pass away. An ocean of grace is always at our disposal. Our lives should be thanksgiving and this will mean a realization that we need not rely so much on ourselves but must look towards him for guidance and strength. We shall cease to worry as to the outcome of our effort, be it success or failure. Our works will be the works of Christ living in us and acting through us. Firm belief in what God is and has done for us, the riches that are *there* for us, enables us to stand erect and hold our heads high, whatever storms swirl around our defenceless head.

No one can pretend that, when besieged as we are by multifarious cares, in time of crushing grief, when dismayed by the horrors of perpetrated evil and the human suffering following on natural disasters, it is easy to maintain a lively sense of God's presence and his love which embraces us at every moment. Yet, to be true to our Christian calling to a life of holiness, to be a light to the world, we must *work* for steadfast faith, or rather, activate the faith we have been given. "This is the work of God, that you believe in the one he has sent" (John 6:29). We must know what we are to believe, and how can we really know with the heart unless we take the responsibility on ourselves to labour to know the one true God and Jesus Christ his Son? Only too easily we fall for an idol that our pride and self-love create. *Reality* is *there* irrespective of our adverting to it or our belief in it. All our blessedness lies in recognizing, affirming and gratefully surrendering to it. In this is God's glory. He made us for this blessedness:

Jesus on the cross proves to be the only accurate picture of God the world has ever seen; and the hands that hold us in existence are pierced with unimaginable nails. God has used every evil done under the sun as the given framework of a new good, by enduring in unchanging love the infinite pain it has caused him.[12]

SEVEN

We Saw His Glory

Deep in his heart for us
The wound of love he bore:
That love wherewith he still inflames
The hearts that him adore.

O Jesus, victim blest,
What else but love divine
Could thee constrain to open thus
That sacred heart of thine?

O fount of endless life,
O spring of water clear,
O flame celestial, cleansing all
Who unto thee draw near![13]

No words are adequate to express the excess of love and heavenly blessings that flow to us from God in the heart of Christ. While we are in this life, we simply could not bear the weight, could not sustain the hurricane of joy that would sweep over us were we even so much as to glimpse it. Such a joy would kill us. We have to be content to live half-blind, dull of heart and hearing, yet always doing our best to receive this love, ready to suffer it in whatever way it comes to us. Our dear God loves us in our spiritual littleness, in "none higher stature than Childhood, in feebleness and failing of might and of wit."[14] In a wonderful way, God is glorified in our non-sublime, un-spiritual state when we entrust ourselves to his love, for "my power is made perfect in weakness" (2 Cor.12: 9)

It is sin that is the cause of our obtuseness and the difficulty we all have in cleaving steadfastly in faith to divine realities, to what is unseen rather than to what is seen. Yet the Church can sing exultingly at the Easter Vigil, "O happy fault of Adam". Therefore with St Paul we have reason to say, "gladly, I boast of my weaknesses, that the power of Christ may rest upon me" (ibid).

Crushingly aware of my own obtuseness, I must press on to stammer as best I can of the gift of God that is Jesus, what he means to us and what it means to live by his life. If we reverently, humbly draw near him and ask him to reveal his heart to us, he will do so in the measure that we can bear it. What we must be convinced of is that when we contemplate Jesus in some incident of his earthly life and commune with him, it is not make-believe but hard reality. Jesus is not some admired, loved figure of the past, our heart's hero about whom we fantasize, but our living Lord, actually present to us, and always life giving. He wants us to "meet" him in the incidents of his earthly life for this is how we get to know him as he is now, and what he wants of us. Rivers of living water flow out from the heart of the Risen Christ.

The first disciples were as dull of heart as we are and it was only through the gift of the Holy Spirit, the Spirit of Truth promised by Jesus as the fruit of his death, that they began to perceive the significance of Jesus' person and especially of his death. To our perception, the passion, death and resurrection of Jesus succeed one another; in reality, they are one single mystery.

The evangelist John makes this clear. The resurrection is not another event following on the death of Jesus but what was happening in his death, the meaning of his death. It is Luke who sets out the mystery chronologically as we celebrate it liturgically. Only when Jesus, obedient unto death, was exalted and endowed with the glory that properly belongs to him as the Word, could the Spirit, the bond of love, the communion between Father and Son, be given to those whom "he was not ashamed to call his brethren"; "the children God has given me" (Heb. 2:12–13).

All of us are familiar with the story of the first Pentecost. Faithful to their Lord's parting command to wait for the "promise of the Father" (Luke 24:49) to endow them with power from on high, the disciples, 120 persons, are praying together on the day of the Jewish feast, when a mighty wind shakes the house, breaking down the walls to sweep through the world. On the head of each praying person, there descends a tongue of fire (Acts 2). The Spirit is given to each one, the Spirit is given to all; the Church is born: that communion of persons, formed by the one Spirit, the Spirit of their Lord. By God's great mercy, we are in that communion, the family of

123

Jesus Christ. The Holy Spirit does not replace Jesus, but brings him to us, to each one of us far more truly and effectively than if we had been with him in his mortal life. It is through the Spirit that everyone in every age has direct contact with the Jesus whom we contemplate in the mysteries of his life: "Christ yesterday, today and the same for ever" (Heb. 13:8).

There is no doubt as to the freedom, the willingness, the earnestness with which Jesus accepted to suffer and die for us: "through the eternal Spirit (he) offered himself to God" for us (cf. Heb. 9:14). "I have compassion on the multitude ... they have nothing to eat, and if I send them away hungry to their homes, they will faint on the way" (Mark 8:2–3). Only Jesus knows our true condition, a starving people, helpless to fend for ourselves in the desert of life. He must do everything for us, be everything for us, our light, our food, our very life, for we have no resources of our own. No one but Jesus can save us and Jesus is there, all readiness, all self-offering to be nothing less than our life-giving Bread. "Having loved his own who were in the world, he loved them to the end", that is, to the uttermost extent of love (John 13:1).

We get the impression, do we not, that the beginning of Jesus' ministry was full of joyous hope. He comes with a message of the Father's love, of a total amnesty for all transgression, a new and glorious beginning if people will hear his word and believe in him. Wherever he goes, he radiates love and hope, preaching and healing. It is very noticeable, especially in the gospel of Matthew, how preaching and healing go together. The healings are outward signs of the inward efficacy of the life-giving word. Only too soon, the dark clouds gather round him.

The people fail to grasp the significance of his miracles. Their enthusiasm for Jesus is merely that for a wonder worker who can satisfy their earthly needs and desires. Following the feeding of the multitude, which the people interpreted as a messianic sign, it reached the dangerous pitch of an attempt to seize him by force and make him king (John 6:1–15). Jesus defuses the crisis by peremptorily ordering his disciples to sail to other side of the lake (Mark 6:45) – how readily they would have fallen in with this popular movement! – and escaping himself into the hills, where he spent the night in prayer, as Mark tells us (Mark 6:46). The people fail to see that such misplaced enthusiasm poses a serious threat to Jesus' life: "the kingdom of heaven is undergoing violence and the violent are taking it away" (Matt. 11:12). It becomes the pretext whereby the Jewish leaders can arraign him before the Roman court. For them, Jesus is a dangerous man, undermining their temporal and spiritual authority, threatening the nation's security under Roman governance and, what is more, claiming a transcendent authority regarding the law and the will of God for Israel.

Ever clear-sighted, Jesus recognizes that the course he is pursuing will lead to his death. "I have not come to do my own will but the will of him who sent me" (John 6:38). The will of his Father is his sole aim, and as the evangelist John makes clear, Jesus is constantly looking to the Father, waiting on his guidance, acting always in obedience to the Father. Success, a manifest achievement is not his aim. At some point – we cannot say just when – he realizes that, contrary to all human ways of thinking, it will be when his voice is silent in death, when the "light" is hidden in the darkness of the tomb (cf. John 12:35–36), that God will triumph and his kingdom come. Even as he evinces this conviction he gives expression to overwhelming grief that it must be so, that the immense love of the Father and all the blessedness that it holds, has been slighted, rejected.

"When the Son of Man comes will he, think you, find faith on earth?" (Luke 18:8). What a sad, troubled heart is here revealed! "If I had not come and spoken to them, they would not have sin; but now they have no excuse for their sin" (John 15:22): sad, sad lament! The love, the tenderness, the compassion he himself has poured out, his tireless service of men, is the very love of the eternal God for hard-hearted, self-centred, frivolous humanity. Only Jesus knows the Father and just what it means to reject the holy love of that most Holy Father. What blessedness his people are refusing, what bitterness, what sorrow creating for themselves! The father prepares a banquet to celebrate the marriage of his son. Everything is joyfully prepared: "All is ready; come, come to the feast."

We know the response: "Sorry, we have more important things on hand." (Cf. Matt. 22:1–11; Luke 14:16–24.) How such blindness must have wrung the heart of Jesus! Every overture of love is rejected, ending in the most terrible of all, the casting out and killing of the beloved Son.

For me, one of the most poignant of Jesus' expressions of grief occurs in Luke's account of the Last Supper. Jesus has been warning the disciples of what lies ahead: he will suffer, shed his blood, be betrayed by one of them. Satan is about to renew his assault on Jesus' holiness. Yet even at this point his disciples' self-interest predominates. What is there in this for them? Who among them is to have precedence in the coming kingdom?

What greater proof of failure than the incomprehension of these men who have lived in such intimacy with him? We can add: what greater proof of the tenacious hold self-interest, the desire to be "somebody", especially a spiritual "somebody", has on the human heart, on our own heart, as a very honest, serious examination will reveal! The Holy Spirit alone can root it out and for this the Son of Man must go on his way, suffer and die.

Jesus recalls the happier days when the disciples could venture forth unprotected, without purse or bag, and safely proclaim his teaching in the towns and villages. That springtime is now past, bitter winter, violence is at hand; their master is to be apprehended as an outlaw and they need a different sort of preparation. Failing completely to grasp his meaning, they produce two swords with which they are prepared to defend him. "It is enough," is Jesus' weary, ironic reply (cf. Luke 22:35–38). He makes no further attempt to enlighten them. All four gospel accounts show that Jesus faced his ordeal alone, his heart broken with disappointment.

Jesus attached enormous importance to the last Passover of his life. He himself, in collaboration with a trusted friend in Jerusalem, chose the place in which he would celebrate it with his disciples. If he were to do so before his arrest, which he knew to be imminent, secrecy was necessary. Earlier in his career, he had given vent to impatient desire for the consummation of the sacrifice of his life, for only then could the Holy Spirit, the fire of God's love sweep through the world: "I have come to spread fire on earth; and would it were already kindled! I have a baptism wherewith I am to be baptised; and how I am straightened until it be accomplished!" (Luke 12:49).

Now, at the supper the same eagerness breaks out: "I have earnestly desired to eat this Passover with you before I suffer; for I tell you I shall not eat it again until it is fulfilled in the kingdom of God" (Luke 22:15–16).

In John's account of the supper, the first thing Jesus does is kneel as a slave to wash the feet of his disciples: "I am among you as a servant." Jesus is God! God our servant! ... Such a word as this, striking an open heart shatters it to pieces. Do we know God at all?, I ask myself. There is only one way in which we can truly know him and that is through Jesus, his perfect image. Jesus' foot washing is a gesture of total self-giving, of loving to the utmost; it has the same significance as the gift of his immolated self under the symbols of bread and wine. In the presence of the friend turned traitor who, at this very moment, is intent on handing him over to his enemies, Jesus hands himself over completely to us in accordance with his Father's will. "I do as the Father has commanded me, so that the world may know that I love the Father" (John 14:31). "Now as they were eating, Jesus took bread, and blessed, and broke it and gave it to his disciples and said, 'Take, eat, this is my body.' And he took a cup, and when he had given thanks he gave it to them saying, 'Drink of it, all of you; for this is my blood of the covenant, which is poured out for many for the forgiveness of sins'" (Matt. 26:26–28). "Do this in remembrance of me" (Luke 22:19) – Jesus' most precious gift to his Church.

With treacherous words, the traitor leaves the supper room of light and love and goes into the night to arrange for Jesus' arrest, and at this moment Jesus exclaims: "Now is the Son of man glorified" (John 13:31); his self-offering is complete. It remains, however, to be enacted in the physical, brutal "breaking" of his sacred body and the pouring out of his blood. When Jesus took bread and wine and made them the symbol of his total self-gift to his disciples, he used the language of sacrifice familiar to them.

They would recall the Day of Atonement when, through the shedding of blood, the covenant was renewed: "This cup which is poured out for you is the new covenant in my blood" (Luke 22:20). The deepest significance of this mystery is that every obstacle between God and man has been destroyed. "Let him kiss me with the kiss of his mouth" (Song 1:2). The new and eternal covenant is established. Jesus in his very person is that covenant, the inseparable, perfect union of God and man. This covenant between God and humankind can never, never be broken.

The salvation achieved in the death and resurrection of Jesus is the centre of human history, indeed of the cosmos, penetrating the farthest reaches of the aeons past, reaching out into the unknown future, the light and life of every human creature that will "receive". Jesus Christ is the one absolute Saviour of the human race and of the entire creation, Prince of the new heaven and the new earth.

No one can give a logical explanation as to just how and why the death of Jesus redeemed us. The New Testament is unanimous in its triumphant proclamation of the fact. Using different images, the writers try to express its meanings, its inexhaustible consequences. None of them claims to give a definitive, clearly reasoned explanation of why that particular way and not some other. It would not occur to them to do so for it would seem presumptuous. Sufficient it is that God, in his love, achieved it in this way.

The wonderful, wonderful fact is that *God took on himself the cost of our "atonement", our "reconciliation" with himself; God "made satisfaction", God put everything right, God leaped the gulf between us and himself and, at dreadful cost, carried us home to himself, God "justified" us, God did for us what we could not do for ourselves.* We can say this: the whole weight of sin and evil – the whole vile armoury of the "prince of this world" (John 14:30) – was hurled in fearful assault against God's love, and was totally defeated. Love triumphed. Love's victory was won, not in the power of the Godhead but in a human frailty, that shrank in revulsion and fear, in quivering humanity that cried to the Father to be spared the ordeal, if it were possible.

The sheep was hopelessly lost. Unable to find its way back to the fold, it lay helpless in the wilderness. The shepherd braves the wilderness and, at cost of great suffering, finds where it lies. The sheep is too blind, too crippled to follow his shepherd; he is not asked to. Joyfully, the shepherd hoists it onto his weary, wounded shoulders and carries it home, exulting. God undertook all the labour of our salvation.

Can we glimpse something of what this means for us? God has done it all for us. We do not have to find ways of atoning, of making satisfaction, of making ourselves righteous and pleasing to God. We cannot take one single step *of ourselves* to draw near to God. God has opened his arms to us. They were always opened but we were blind, stubborn, crippled. He sent out his Word to heal us: Jesus, the divine Word, came as our servant, our shepherd, our saviour to carry us back to the Father's heart: Come and share your master's joy:

> O crucified Lord, we kneel in utter
>   reverence;
> O glorious risen Saviour, we exult in your
>   triumph;
> You died in pain
> to bring the whole created world into
>   your joy.[15]

"In this was the love of God made manifest among us, that God sent his only Son into the world so that we might have life through him. In this is love, not that we first loved God, but that he loved us and sent his Son to be the expiation of our sins" (1 John 4:9–10). O mystery of inexpressible love!

Many years ago, I came across a little French parable that moved me deeply, a parable of unbreakable sacrificial love. A widowed mother had an only son whom she cherished. Her tireless loving care was repaid with ingratitude. Heartless wretch that he was, heedless of her needs, time and again he left her, only to return when his pockets were empty and he was hungry. Each time, she would welcome him and supply his needs at cost to herself. Eventually, his selfish greed had stripped her of everything she had. On his return and finding her unable to give him what he wanted, he was furious and in anger tore her heart from her breast and in sheer contempt threw it on the ground. As he ran to the door, he fell over the heart, and the heart said: "Have you hurt yourself, my son?"

"Let him kiss me with the kiss of his mouth" (Song 1:1). In the truest meaning of the word we can speak, not merely of a loving relationship with God, but of union with him. In principle, we are taken with our risen Lord into the very heart of the Trinity. It is given to us to know God even as God knows himself. We are not merely called his children but actually are his "offspring". Whereas adoption here on earth is a legal matter and one of chosen love and acceptance only, in divine adoption the divine life-stream flows through us. As Jesus shared our flesh and blood in the time of his kenosis, now that he is glorified we share his divine life, a life that belongs to no creature by nature, but is proper to God alone. This life comes to us through Christ.

To say Christ is our representative and all he did was as our representative is inadequate. More is involved. In a way, we cannot fully grasp we are "in" Christ, incorporated in him. God has given him to us as our High Priest, as our Head and, in solidarity with him, "through him, with him and in him" we are able to offer God perfect atonement, perfect worship, a love that is worthy of him. So it is that through God's wonderful devising, it was man, one of us, who by his unparalleled, humble, unswerving obedience brought us home to our God and our Father:

> O wisest love! that flesh and blood
> Which did in Adam fail,
> Should strive afresh against the foe,
> Should strive and should prevail.[16]

"(God) is the source of your life in Christ Jesus, whom God made our wisdom, our righteousness and sanctification and redemption" (1 Cor. 1:30). All is *gift*. Nothing is wanting to us. We have been given the right to a marvellous inheritance, nothing less than the inheritance of Christ: "all that is mine is yours" (Luke 15:31); "the glory which thou has given to me I have given to them" (John 17:22); "heirs of God and joint heirs with Christ" (Rom. 8:17), can we even begin to penetrate the implications of this? People of deep prayer and some theologians have used the bold term "deification" as the only adequate way of expressing this work of God. The human self has to "die" in the sense that it must surrender completely to the divine embrace. This divine embrace purifies and transforms it. God works, and God's work is God.

Only when we have died with Christ, been buried with him, and risen with him, will we be truly human. Now we are in the process of becoming. "Behold the Man", God says to us through the mouth of Pilate. Jesus alone is *the* man, truly human as God created us to be. Our task is to enter into the kingdom prepared for us before the foundation of the world (cf. Matt. 25:34).

EIGHT

So Tender, So Compassionate

Come to me, all who labour and are
     heavy laden,
and I will give you rest.
Take my yoke upon you, and learn from
     me,
for I am gentle and lowly of heart,
and you will find rest for your souls.
For my yoke is easy, and my burden is
     light. (Matt. 11: 28–30)

Jesus sees that we carry a burden we are not meant to carry and bear a yoke that galls our spirits. "Come to me," he says, "learn from me and you will cast off that burden and the yoke that does not fit, and take up my burden, shoulder my yoke, and find rest." Learn from me – from no one else – what it is to be meek and humble of heart. Learn what it is to be the Father's beloved child.

In the synoptic gospels, only when quoting the *Shema* of Israel's faith, does Jesus say we must love God. He says we must fear God, that is, we must hold him in profound reverence and awe, and we must trust him. It is our neighbour we must love.

A fine distinction is being made. It is within our power to love our neighbour as ourselves; we are dealing with an equal to whose welfare we must attend. Jesus seems to be saying that we cannot love and serve God in the same sort of way in which we love and serve our neighbour, while assuring us that everything we do for others is done to him.

We do not serve God, do things for his benefit,

do not give him something he has not got. Obviously not, and yet, perversely, frequently our attitudes and actions assume that we can and must do exactly that. We overlook the fact that God himself in Jesus has told us that he does not want us to serve him; he wants to serve us. This is clearly demonstrated in the gospel accounts where Jesus goes around healing, feeding, comforting, succouring, teaching. When he welcomes his faithful ones to the heavenly banquet, he will be there with his apron on ready to serve them (cf. Luke 12:37). It is shown too in his judgment on the behaviour of the two sisters, Martha and Mary (Luke 10:38–42).

Jesus comes as a guest and Martha sets about serving him while Mary simply sits at his feet and listens to him. She assumes the role of the disciple. Martha is intent on feeding Jesus; Mary is intent on letting Jesus feed her. Martha is irritated: her sister's behaviour is selfish, Jesus is condoning it and failing to appreciate her own loving service. Were Jesus an ordinary guest, Martha's complaint would be justified, but Jesus is not an ordinary guest and this Mary realizes. Mary understood that Jesus does not come into our house to be served but to be allowed to serve. The greatest honour we can show him is to let him do so. It would seem that at the very end of Jesus' life, Mary realized that he was to die and that *he must be allowed to die*. She did not cry out against the obtuseness of his disciples and friends, urging them to act, to get him away from danger. Her reaction is the opposite of Peter's "You shall never wash my feet!" (John 13:8).

Mary knows that he must die for her and for every human person; otherwise, they can have no part with him. She does what she can; she pours over his head a costly perfume proclaiming him as king and anointing him for his burial. "What a waste!" onlookers exclaimed. Jesus alone knew the profound significance of this act and ordained that wherever the gospel was preached this woman and her action should be recalled so that his disciples would thereby penetrate his own heart's love for humankind (Matt. 26:6–13; Mark 14:3–11; John 12:1–8).

Nothing so glorifies God, so pleases him as our trust. I know many people who say simply and sincerely that they love God and their lives prove that this is not mere sentiment. For myself, I have never been able to say it. It has seemed

143

presumptuous for me to do so, claiming a sort of proportionality between God and me. Most certainly, I have wanted to love him and it has been and is my belief, my hope and my confidence that, when his work in me is complete, I will love him because I will love with the heart of Christ.

It is hard, at least for me, to detach the word "love" from feeling and in my case feelings of love, generally speaking, have been absent. Still I maintain that trust includes everything and is infinitely pleasing to God. It *is* love in that it is yearning desire for what the heart lacks, coupled with confidence that its desire will be fulfilled. It is adoration and pure worship, for it acknowledges God for what he is, infinite fidelity and love. It is a practical avowal that we have absolutely nothing as of ourselves, that everything, everything, whatsoever it may be, is all from him, is all gift. It is affirming the absoluteness of God and his absolute claim on the human heart.

Trust takes God at his word, trusting that word beyond every subjective emotion and experience, beyond everything that seems to contradict it, against all temptation from within or without.

Trust is implicit thanksgiving. "We give you thanks for your great glory", is the cry of the trusting heart. The trust I mean is inseparable from faith and hope. It is not just intellectual assent to a statement of faith, it is a surrender of self to God. It is the human answer to God's revelation of himself, to his utter reliability and his steadfast loving kindness towards us. It is the answer God has longed for down the ages and has so rarely received. One has given it and in our name: Jesus, the great "Amen" (Rev. 3:14; cf. 2 Cor. 1:19–20).

"Truly I say to you, unless you turn and become like children, you will never enter the kingdom of heaven" (Matt. 18:3). Jesus was always the child. A child is totally dependent on its parents for simply everything. Instinctively it knows it is unimportant, knows it is helpless and without resources of any kind; and, again instinctively, is utterly sure that, preciously loved as it is, it will be cared for. Jesus is telling us that we must *choose* to trust the Father with the same absolute, unquestioning trust a child has by instinct in its parents. To do this consistently throughout our life is the hardest thing possible. "Narrow is the gate and strait is the way that leads to life and few there are that find it" (Matt. 7:14). We must "strive" to enter by this narrow gate (cf. Luke 13:24). Jesus is this narrow gate, Jesus in his lowly humanity, in his full acceptance of that humanity in its weakness, its suffering and its mortality.

The writer of the Letter to the Hebrews is emphatic that Jesus was tempted, as we are tempted, to avoid the full implications of being "man" not God. The "temptations in the desert" give a compressed picture of what was, for Jesus, a recurring temptation throughout his ministry. It came from without: give us a sign that will convince us of the truth of your claims; show yourself to the world; do not go on about betrayal, suffering and death, God won't let such things happen to you! Even to the end the people and even his disciples "watched" to see if there would be some heavenly intervention. His enemies mocked his helplessness and degradation. Jesus' eyes were always on his Father. Nothing would deter him from doing his Father's will and it was to the Father he surrendered his life and his mission. The basic obedience demanded of Jesus was the same as ours: to accept fully the vocation to be human. We are shown him praying to his Father "with loud cries and tears" (Heb. 5:7–8), his heart ready to break with grief, beside himself with dread of what lay before him, so overcome that he fell prostrate on the ground and prayed to be spared. But, "not my will but yours be done" (Mark 14:33–42).

He is our pioneer, our leader in faith and trust and it is from his surrender that we draw strength to do what of ourselves we cannot do. It seems we must surrender that which we feel makes us human. Revelation has shown us something we could not otherwise have known, that we are called not merely to a splendid human destiny of a kind we can appreciate and that, with God's help, we can gradually achieve, but to one that transcends any created nature whatsoever. We are called to share God's own life. We were created to receive uncreated life. Yet our nature, along with every creature that we know of on our planet, has an innate drive towards a fulfilment that is within its powers to attain. We humans are the only creatures who know they must die. Without faith's vision, human life is tragic. "It were no boon to have been born had we not been redeemed."[17] All we have done to develop ourselves and the world around us eventually comes to nothing. We think of persons whom we have known and loved making a beautiful thing of their life, and must all this beauty, this mature love come to naught? Here lies the core of our human drama. *To come to our transcendent destiny we must renounce the powerful natural instinct to achieve a destiny by our own powers.*

We are open ended, a potentiality, a capacity for God, and when we allow ourselves to confront the reality of ourselves, we experience *emptiness, want, desire*. Ours is an incredibly wonderful vocation but a difficult one that involves an inescapable tension. On the one hand, we must accept our poverty, which is the sign or sacrament of our transcendence; acknowledging that, of ourselves, we can never attain our end. "Who then can be saved?" exclaimed the bewildered Peter. "It is impossible for man, but not for God for everything is possible to God" (Matt. 19:25–26; Mark 10:26–27; Luke 18:26–27). On the other hand, we are summoned to a great moral effort, conforming our lives to the demands of the gospel. Our natural powers must be developed to the full and we must devote ourselves to cooperating with God in the transformation of creation.

Earth is not a spiritual gymnasium in which we exercise ourselves to fit us out for heaven. The created world has a value in itself and its destiny is linked with our own. As we throw ourselves into this holy endeavour, we shall experience disappointments, humiliations and, often, failure. The shoddiness of our Christian living can press painfully on us and from the depths of our hearts we shall know that we are "unprofitable servants" (Luke 17:9–10). This fact we must humbly accept and with it the awareness that nothing we do brings God down to us. However, the important thing is that our effort, and, above, all our holy trusting, makes us *there* for him to come to us. All our trust must be based, not on what we do, not on what appears, not on achievements but on the absoluteness of Christ's victory. We can be confident that nothing whatever is lost or wasted, it is "treasure in heaven" (cf. Matt. 6:19–21; Luke 12:32–34): not heaven understood as hereafter, but heaven as God's realm, God's view of things, God's "eternal life" that even now envelops and permeates our mortal existence.

Only if we know Jesus can we hope to have such trust. How can we know him unless we go to him? How can we learn from him to be meek and

149

humble of heart unless we live close to his heart? Vital it is to feed on the riches of his house! Each one of us is responsible for doing so. Each one of us must take the trouble, really labour to know our Saviour, pray, long to know him: "Show me your face, reveal your heart to me!"

We must read, we must think, we must ponder deeply. Nothing less than the ultimate is at stake. Have we to admit that we are intellectually lazy when it comes to divine realities, to things that do not make an impact on the senses? Well-worn platitudes, interpretations of Jesus' words, of his parables and actions that we imbibed long ago are substituted for real knowledge and we are satisfied. Is it not a sacred duty of ordained ministers to acquire a profound, prayerful knowledge of the glorious truths of revelation so as to enlighten, encourage and inspire the faithful who perhaps have not the same resources to hand?

What God longs for is a childlike trust that will surrender us to his love. "Do what you will with me" (cf. Luke 1:38); give me an attentive, directed heart and mind that ceaselessly asks, "what do you want of me?" (cf. Acts 22:10). God is then free to work within us, bringing to bear on each one of us "the immeasurable greatness of his power", that "great might which he accomplished in Christ when he raised him from the dead and made him sit at his right hand in the heavenly places" (Eph. 1:19–20). Let God work; it is *love* that works and his work is love.

Transformation necessarily calls for purification: dross must be burned away; there must be a dying to our self-centred selves in order to live with the life of Jesus. It is when God is drawing close that so many of us turn back, or at least, stand still. Maybe a little parable will illustrate the paradox. We are given the task of making a lamp for God to shine in. We set to work in earnest, in devotional exercises, in serving our neighbour, developing ourselves and, in a word, doing all the good that lies in our power. Then we ask: "What is yet wanting?" The answer comes: "Now carry your lantern up the mountain to offer it to me."

So, carrying our precious, beautifully crafted lantern that has cost so much labour, we set out. As we progress, mysteriously, our lamp loses its lustre. Why, it is tawdry! So tawdry, in fact, that we are tempted to run back to make another or embellish the one in our hands. Many do yield to this impulse and, alas, spend their lives making their lantern beautiful so as to be worthy of God. Others, possibly only a few, go on, painfully aware of the pathetic nature of what they are offering, but they think to themselves: God can shine in anything; his shining will be the more evident in this poor, misshapen tin than in a bejewelled lamp of gold. So, trustingly, on they trudge, thinking more of God than of their gift. It may then come to pass that a dark cloud overshadows them and a voice from the cloud says: "Now, drop your lantern."

Narrow is the gate, strait the way that leads to life, it allows for no baggage, no spiritual acquisitions and no swollen self-importance. It is for the "little ones".

"How hard it is for the rich man to enter the kingdom of heaven!" (Matt. 19:23–24; Mark 10:23–26; Luke 8:23–25). There are different forms of riches and not the least obstructive are what we might call spiritual riches. The natural impulse to do it ourselves, the innate assumption that we can ourselves achieve our destiny, operates subtly, unrecognized in our spiritual life. I doubt if any one of us has always, from the start, kept to the strait way. The Lord has to work deeply within us before we are slim enough to get through the narrow door. It is when we are engaged in prayer that we are likely to be made aware of our spiritual inadequacy, indeed of our destitution.

We think of prayer as something we do for God whereas prayer is essentially a gift. Prayer is intimacy with God and it is God who offers us this intimacy. We respond. There is only one Christian prayer and that is Jesus, the New and Eternal Covenant, the union in person of God and man. All Christian prayer is essentially through him, with him and in him. That we should pray is as much a command of the Lord as that we must love our neighbour. Further, our prayer must be "in my name". "Truly, truly, I say to you, if you ask anything of the Father, he will give it to you in my name. Hitherto you have asked nothing in my name; ask and you will receive, that your joy may be full" (John 16:23–24).

The implications of this simple command are immeasurably profound. If we ponder it carefully, we shall see that it must eliminate any claim to a spiritual competence of our own and, consequently, remove the burden of anxiety we feel at our helplessness and incompetence – a "burden" that is *not* the Lord's. The God revealed in Jesus is like a loving mother who, seeing her little one struggling to climb the stairs to reach her, runs down and lifts up the child to her heart. If only we believed! If only we took God at his word, how serenely we would go!

Jesus himself gave us his own prayer, a prayer to Abba, my dear, dear Father. In the early centuries of the Church, the Lord's Prayer had a sacramental significance. It was *the* Christian prayer, and not until the Liturgy on Wednesday of the fourth week of Lent was it solemnly handed to the catechumens. Do we reverence it? Reflection shows that it contains all that God wants for us, all the intentions of his divine heart.

The Eucharist is the most complete expression of the content of the Lord's Prayer. It is from the perfect self-offering of Jesus, his perfect obedience, that all good flows. The Eucharist is the supreme Christian prayer and it is not of our making, it is *given*. Can we measure the spiritual efficacy of the Eucharist and of the Lord's Prayer prayed in faith? Where Christ is, there is his Body, the whole Church. Whether in the splendid setting of a cathedral or in a humble parish church with small resources, the sacred Liturgy, celebrated with faith and union of hearts, is the greatest of all prayers. In liturgical worship, we are more than ourselves, we are the praying Church, so it does not matter if emotionally we cannot "rise to the occasion" or cannot identify with the sentiments we are expressing.

There is no such thing as *my* prayer. When we set aside some time each day exclusively to pray in the solitude of our heart, even then we are not alone but united to the whole Church. The Spirit of Christ within us prompts us to pray and prays within us. What confidence this should give us, especially when our prayer seems so shoddy, hardly prayer at all. If we really believe that prayer is essentially God at work, purifying, transforming us, then we will not get discouraged when it is drab and dry. It is not easy to accept in a practical way the self-revelation that is given us in real prayer.

We begin to see all manner of selfish elements that hitherto had seemed innocent. Is there one motive in all we do that is utterly pure? How spiritually obtuse we are! Fidelity to this kind of unsatisfactory prayer is costly but it is asked of us. Let us beware of the subtle temptation to flee from it and seek out some more satisfactory way of prayer, a way of doing it better that will assure us that we really are praying. Whom are we trying to satisfy? We cannot make ourselves holy and clean and pleasing to God. "You alone are the Holy One."[18] Holiness is of God, it is the work of God. The Holy Spirit must take us into the holiness of Jesus. We cannot have a holiness that is "mine".

There seems to me a danger today of prayerful people misunderstanding the nature of prayer and confusing it with self-development. Many Christians are adopting techniques of self-calming or "centring" drawn from diverse sources outside the Christian tradition. The disciplines involved are undoubtedly beneficial and, persevered in, effect personal integration and a sense of harmony and peace. Good as they are in themselves, they are no substitute for prayer, for the humble, trustful, childlike, naked exposure of self to God, that looks only to him to purify us to our depths, to eliminate from our hearts the deep, deep roots of self-seeking which we cannot see, let alone eradicate. This work of God can be painful, even frightening, but to run away from it is running away from God.

Does it not become clear to us that we must base our lives, not on anything within ourselves or anything within this world but on the great and glorious promises of God?

Although we do not admit this to ourselves, as often as not we are relying on what we feel, what things seem like, on "my" prayer, "my" goodness, "my" faithful service. Jesus offers us joy, freedom, rest in throwing off the burden of self-reliance and self-achieving to lie surrendered in our Father's arms. Trust, humility, obedience, these are the great Christ-like virtues for which we must entreat and, insofar as we can, work. These are the human dispositions whereby we enter the kingdom of heaven, a kingdom of untold riches, not available to the senses but more real than everything we experience as real. Constantly, Jesus speaks of entering into something that is already there and there for us. It will be there whether we enter or not, for in no way does it depend on us, but on the pure, gratuitous love of our Creator, Saviour God. So tender, so compassionate is the Lord; patient and unwearied is the love of his heart.

We have a choice: *to believe* the God who has shown himself to us, deny self and its subjectivity, which, of course dominates our consciousness, drop our "lantern", surrender and plunge into the holy mist, or we can go on clinging to self, fashioning a holiness of our own which, with its illusions, its fears and burdens, cannot glorify the Father. The choice is ours:

> With all my heart, Lord, I long for you;
> take me in your arms and keep me safe.
> (cf. Ps. 25(24):1–2; Mark 9:36; 10:16)

NOTES

1 Julian of Norwich, *Revelations of Divine Love* c. VII.
2 Ibid. c. VI.
3 A Prayer of St Richard of Chichester.
4 Julian of Norwich, *Revelations of Divine Love* c. IV.
5 Ibid. c. XXVIII.
6 See n. 2.
7 Sr Wendy Becket, *The Burning Men*.
8 Hilaire Belloc, *Courtesy*.
9 William Wordsworth, *Intimations of Immortality from Recollections of Early Childhood*.
10 Richard Crashaw, *At the Nativity*.
11 Ursula Goodenough, *The Sacred Depths of Nature*.
12 John Austin Baker, *The Foolishness of God*.
13 To Christ the Prince of Peace, *Catholicum Hymnologium Germanicum 1587* translated by Edward Caswell.
14 Julian of Norwich, *Revelations of Divine Love* c. LXIV (see also LX–XIII).
15 Antiphon from the Divine Office of Good Friday.
16 John Henry Newman, *Praise to the Holiest in the Height*.
17 Vigil of Easter, *The Exsultet*.
18 *Gloria in Excelsis Deo*.